Wyoming Historical Trivia

J. J. Hammond

Wyoming Historical Trivia

J. J. Hammond

© 2011 by J.J. Hammond
Edited by Jean Henry Mead
All rights reserved, including those to reproduce this book, or parts thereof, in any form, without written permission of the publisher.

ISBN: 978-1-931415-26-2

First printing, December 2004
Second printing, May 2005,
Third printing, December 2011
Printed in the United States

Cover design of Jeremiah Johnson's gravesite, Old Trail Town in Cody Wyoming

Books by Medallion:

Westerners: Candid and Historic Interviews
Wyoming's Cowboy Poets and Their Poetry
Casper Country: Wyoming's Heartland
Wyoming Historical Trivia
Escape, a Wyoming Historical Novel
Diary of Murder
A Village Shattered
Murder on the Interstate
Mystery of Spider Mountain
Ghost of Crimson Dawn

Medallion Books
Glenrock, Wyoming

Dedicated to:

Bob and Jennifer Hammond

Table of Contents

Wyoming's Vital Statistics	1
Wyoming "Firsts"	9
Prehistoric Wyoming	21
Wyoming's Native Americans	29
Explorers and Mountain Men	33
Forts and Battlefields	45
Wyoming Outlaws	53
Homesteading	61
Cattle and Cattle Wars	65
Ghost Towns	71
Cities and Towns	79
Wyoming Counties	89
Wyoming Water	101
Wyoming Mountains	107
Wyoming Historic Sites	115
National Parks, Forests, Monuments	121
Wyoming State Parks	127
Early Communications and Newspapers	133
Wyoming Disasters	159
Modes of Transportation	165
Wyoming Representatives	171

Wyoming's Vital Statistics

How did the name Wyoming originate?

The name Wyoming has been attributed to two sources. In the Algonquin language the name means "land of the vast plains." The Delaware Indian meaning is "alternating mountains and valleys."

In which year did Wyoming become a territory?

Wyoming Territory was formally organized by an Act of Congress July 25, 1868, from the western portion of Dakota Territory and eastern sections of Idaho and Utah territories.

When did Wyoming become a state?

Wyoming Territory was admitted to the union on July 10, 1890, as the 44th united state.

If Alaska ranks first in size and Rhode Island is this country's smallest state, what is Wyoming's ranking?

Wyoming's 97,914 square miles rank as the ninth largest state in the union.

Where is Wyoming's state capital?

Cheyenne is located in the southeastern corner of the state in Laramie County.

What does the Great Seal represent?

The central figure holds a staff-bearing banner which represents the state's motto: "Equal Rights." Others represent the mining and livestock industries. Wyoming's entry as a state is represented by the numbers 44 on a five-pointed star. Lamps that burn with the Light of Knowledge sit atop the pillars and scrolls that circle the twin pillars. They contain the names of Wyoming's most important industries: oil, livestock, mining and agriculture. The state's designation as a territory and the dates of entry as a state are also included in the design: 1868 and 1890. The second legislature adopted the Great Seal in 1893.

Who designed the Wyoming Flag?

Verna Keyes of Casper designed the flag which was adopted by the fourteenth legislature in 1917. Mrs. Keyes, a Buffalo, Wyoming, native, designed the red, white and blue flag with the state's Great Seal in the center of a white bison. The bison represents the former monarch of the plains; the red border symbolizes the Native Americans who depended on the herds for sustenance. Red also represents the pioneers who died attempting to reclaim the land. The white border represents purity; the blue symbolizes the Wyoming skies as well as justice and virility.

What is the state fossil?

The knightia, a reddish, herring-like fish, was adopted as the state fossil in 1987. The fossil was discovered in the Green River Formation in 1840.

Which are Wyoming's largest cities, as of the 2010 census?

> Cheyenne: 59,466
> Casper: 55,316,
> Laramie: 30,816,
> Gillette: 29,084,
> Rock Springs: 23,036,
> Sheridan: 17,044,
> Green River: 12,515,
> Evanston: 12,359,
> Riverton: 10,615
> Jackson: 9, 577.

Where is Wyoming's highest mountain peak?

Gannett Peak, at 13,804 feet, is located in the northern Wind River Range on the Continental Divide in west-central Wyoming. It's situated in both Sublette and Fremont counties about 25 miles north-northeast of the town of Pinedale.

Where is the state's lowest point of land?

The Belle Fourche River in the northeastern corner of the state is 3,100 feet above sea level.

Which is Wyoming's adopted flower?

The Indian paintbrush (Castilleja linariaefolia) was adopted as the state's flower in 1917.

Which species is Wyoming's state bird?

The meadowlark was designated as the state bird in 1927.

What is the official state dinosaur?

Triceratops, one of the largest dinosaurs to roam the high plains, was designated as the state's official dinosaur in 1994.

What is Wyoming's state tree?

The plains cottonwood was adopted as the state tree.

Which animal is the state mammal?

The bison was adopted by the state legislature

in 1985.

What is the state fish?

The cutthroat trout was designated as the state fish in 1987.

Which gemstone represents Wyoming?

Jade, or nephrite, was adopted as the state gemstone in 1967.

Which reptile represents Wyoming?

The horned toad was selected as the state reptile in 1967.

Who were the territorial governors?

John Campbell, R, Apr. 15, 1869-Mar.1, 1875
John Thayer, R, March 1, 1875-May 29, 1878
John Hoyt, R, May 29, 1878-Aug. 22, 1882
William Hale, R, Aug. 22, 1882-Jan. 13, 1885
*ESN Morgan R, Jan. 13, 1885-Feb. 28, 1885
Francis E. Warren, R, Feb. 28, 1885-Jan. 11, 1886
George Baxter, D, Jan. 11, 1886-Dec. 20, 1886
*E.S.N. Morgan, R, Dec. 20, 1886-Jan. 24, 1887
Thomas Moonlight, D, Jan. 24, 1887-April 9, 1889
Francis E. Warren R, April 9, 1889-November 11, 1890

*Acting governor

J. J. Hammond

Who were the governors and when did they serve?

Francis E. Warren, R, Nov.11-Nov. 24, 1890
Amos Barber, R, Nov. 24, 1890-Jan. 2, 1893
John E. Osborn, R, Jan. 2, 1893-Jan. 7, 1895
William Richards, R, Jan. 7, 1895-Jan. 2, 1889
DeForest Richards, R, Jan 21, 1899-Apr. 28, 1903
Fennimore Chatterman, R, Apr. 28, 1903-Jan. 2, 1905
Bryant B. Brooks, D, Jan. 2, 1905- Jan. 2, 1911
Joseph M. Carey, D, Jan. 2, 1911-Jan. 4, 1915
John B. Kendrick, D, Jan. 4, 1915-Feb. 26, 1917
Frank Houx, D, Feb. 26, 1917-Jan. 6, 1919
Robert D. Carey, R, Jan. 6, 1919- Jan. 1, 1923
William B. Ross, D, Jan. 1, 1923-Oct. 2, 1924
Frank Lucas, R, Oct. 2, 1924-Jan. 5, 1925
Nellie Tayloe Ross, D, Jan. 5, 1925-Jan. 3, 1927
Frank C. Emerson, R, Jan. 3, 1927-Feb. 18, 1931
Alonzo M. Clark, R, Feb. 18, 1931-Jan. 2, 1933
Leslie A. Miller, D, Jan. 2, 1933-Jan. 2, 1939
Nels H. Smith, R, Jan. 2, 1939- Jan. 4, 1943
Lester C. Hunt, R, Jan. 4, 1943-Jan. 3, 1949
Arthur G. Crane, R, Jan. 3, 1949-Jan. 1, 1951
Frank A. Barrett, R, Jan. 1, 1951-Jan. 3, 1953
C.J. "Doc" Rogers, R, Jan. 3, 1953-Jan. 3, 1955
Milward Simpson, R, Jan. 3, 1955-Jan. 5, 1959
J.J. "Joe" Hickey, D, Jan. 5, 1959-Jan. 1, 1961
Jack R. Gage, D, Jan. 1, 1961-Jan. 7, 1963
Clifford Hansen, R, Jan. 7, 1963-Jan. 2, 1967
Stanley K. Hathway, R, Jan. 2, 1967-Jan. 6, 1975
Ed Herschler, D, Jan. 6, 1975-Jan. 5, 1987

Mike Sullivan, D, Jan. 5, 1987-Jan. 2, 1995
Jim Geringer, R, Jan. 2, 1995-Jan. 6, 2003
David Freuedenthal, D, Jan. 6, 2003-Jan 3, 2011
Matthew "Matt" Mead, R, Jan. 2, 2011—

Wyoming "Firsts"

Who first introduced a bill to create Wyoming Territory?

In 1865, Ohio Congressman James M. Ashley introduced a bill to the thirty-eighth Congress to create Wyoming Territory, but it failed to pass both houses. Three years later, Illinois Senator Richard Yates introduced a bill that carved the territory from eastern Utah, western Dakota Territory, and eastern Idaho. President Grover Cleveland approved the new territory.

Who is credited with the first discovery of South Pass, Wyoming?

Robert Stuart, a member of the Astor party led by William Price Hunt, left Michigan in 1810 for Oregon. On the return trip, Stuart left Oregon with sixty men, ten canoes, and two barges, following the original trail east. They crossed the Teton Mountains as well as South Pass, where Indians and mountain men had previously traveled. Stuart, however, was given credit for the discovery.

Who were the first women in the nation to be given the right to vote?

A bill granting Wyoming women the right to vote was signed into law by John A. Campbell, the first territorial governor, on December 10, 1869, but a Utah woman, Sarah Young, was the first in the country to legally cast her ballot on February 14, 1870. Utah Territorial Legislature passed its suffrage law on February 10, 1870, and its women voted four days later, although they were not allowed to hold office. Wyoming women voted for the first time in August 1870, and were allowed to hold office.

Who was the first woman speaker of the Wyoming House of Representatives?

Edness Kimball Wilkins was elected speaker of the Wyoming House in 1966. The twenty-five year legislator was honored with a state park, established in Natrona County in her name.

Who served as this nation's first woman justice of the peace?

Esther Hobart Morris was appointed to her post in 1870 in Laramie City, the year after

Wyoming women were granted the right to vote. Her family moved to Wyoming Territory for the purpose of mining gold, and after she married, she settled in South Pass City. There she was appointed a delegate to the Republican national convention held in Cleveland, Ohio, in 1895. Esther Morris was also an honored guest in Cheyenne to celebrate Wyoming's statehood in 1890.

Who was the world's first woman bailiff?

Mary Atkinson of Albany County, Wyoming, was appointed to her job in 1870.

Who became Wyoming's first woman engineer?

Grace Raymond Hebard graduated with an engineering degree from The University of Iowa. She arrived in Laramie in 1891 to work as the only female draftsman in Cheyenne, a job she held for eight years. During that period she also earned a correspondence course master's degree in literature from Iowa State. She was then hired as secretary for the University of Wyoming's Board of Trustees. In that capacity, she earned a PhD in political science from Wesleyan University through correspondence courses and became an economics and political science professor at University of Wyoming. The Wyoming District Court granted her the right in 1917 to issue citizenship certificates to students who passed her immigration course, which empowered her as a federal authority agent. Although her own state had already granted women the right to vote, Hebard championed the cause of national women's suffrage throughout the nation. She was also a championship golfer and the author of a number of western history books.

Where did this nation's first all-women jury serve?

Jurors were sworn in on March 7, 1870, in the town of Laramie.

Which woman was the first appointed to the Wyoming Supreme Court?

The first woman Supreme Court justice for the state of Wyoming was Marilyn Kite in 2000.

Which Wyoming town was governed entirely by women?

Jackson was governed from 1920 until 1921 by women. Grace Miller was elected mayor and Rose Crabtree defeated her husband Henry, the former mayor, for a city council seat. Also elected to the council were Mae Deloney, Genevieve Van Vleck, and Fautina Haight. Other women that year to serve the town were Pearl Williams, who was elected as the town marshal; Edna Huff as the Jackson health officer, Marta Winger as the town clerk; and Viola Lumbeck as treasurer.

Wyoming Historical Trivia

Who was the first woman president of the Wyoming state senate?

April Brimmer Kunz was the first woman to be elected president of the state senate in 2002.

Which national monument was the first to be designated?

Devil's Tower is one of Wyoming's most visited tourist attractions and was the setting for the film, "Close Encounters of the Third Kind." The monolith, which resembles a huge petrified stump, is 600 feet in elevation and located in the northeastern section of Wyoming in the Black Hills area. President Theodore Roosevelt designated the monument in 1906.

Which president designated Yellowstone as the United States' first national Park?

In 1872, President Ulysses S. Grant designated more than two million acres of land in the northwest corner of Wyoming and portions of eastern Idaho, and southern Montana. The largest park in the world contains thousands of thermal springs and geysers as well as nearly 300 species of birds and animals.

Which national forest was the first to be established in the U.S.?

The 2.4 million acre Shoshone National Forest was created in 1891 as part of the Yellowstone Forest Reserve. Buffalo Bill's Camp Monaco was established in the heavily wooded area of the forest, where royalty camped while taking part in Cody's last big game hunt in 1913. President Benjamin Harrison signed an act into law in 1891 to create the first of Wyoming's nine national forests as well as the nation's first.

Who was the first woman Hereford cattle judge?

Ruth Geier Rice was not only the first woman Hereford cattle judge, she served as the first woman Sheridan County commissioner and was the first woman to serve on the county planning commission. She was also nominated to the Northern International Livestock Exposition Hall of Fame with seven men from the U.S. and Canada in 1980, following the deaths of both her husband and only son in separate plane crashes. Rice held the large business together on her own.

Who was the first woman elected to a Wyoming state office?

Estelle Reel, a Laramie school teacher, assumed the post of Superintendent of Public Instruction in an 1894 landslide election.

Where were the first coal mines in Wyoming?

Two mines opened in Carbon County in 1868,

Wyoming Historical Trivia

the same year the Union Pacific Railroad was routed through the area. The town of Carbon was established some fifteen miles south of Medicine Bow that year. Seven coal mines were in operation by 1902, when the mines were closed following retrieval of 347 tons of ore.

Where was the first forest ranger station in the nation established?

Shoshone National Forest's Wapiti Ranger Station was established about 30 miles west of Cody, Wyoming, in 1903. It was named for the elk herds that inhabit the area of northwestern Wyoming.

Where was this nation's first county public library system located?

The Laramie County Library System was organized during August 1886.

Where was Wyoming's first oil well located?

Excavated in 1884 with picks and shovels by Mike Murphy and his cohorts, Tar Springs in Fremont County was the site of the state's first oil well. The site was discovered in 1832 by Captain B. L. E. Bonneville, who reported the tar springs long known to the Indians. The French-Cheyenne Lajeunesse brothers sold the grease to emigrants traveling the Oregon-Mormon trails for lubricants and medicinal purposes.

When was gold first discovered in Wyoming?

In 1842, seven years before the California gold rush, the yellow metal was discovered near the Wind River Mountains in what came to be known as South Pass City. The first nuggets were found by a Georgia trapper who was later found scalped with a bag of nuggets hanging from his neck. Gold seekers had been warned by mountain man, Jim Bridger, to be wary of hostile natives in the area.

Where was the first artificially lighted football game held in Wyoming?

The first interscholastic football game to take place under artificial lights was in the town of Midwest in 1925.

Which Wyoming woman doctor was the first to practice in the state?

Lillian Heath Nelson was one of three Rawlins doctors in 1881 to perform an autopsy on outlaw George Manuse, aka "Big Nose" George Parrott. The autopsy was performed by cutting off the top of the outlaw's skull to determine, they said, any criminal abnormalities. None apparently was found. Lillian Heath Nelson reportedly studied obstetrics with a Rawlins, Wyoming, doctor.

Who owned the West's first polo field?

Wyoming Historical Trivia

Oliver Wallop and Malcolm Moncrief laid out the first polo field in the Big Horn, Wyoming area to accommodate British army officers who wanted the horses they purchased ridden the length of the field to judge their gaits. Wallop and Moncrief sold horses to the British for the Boer War (1899-1902), and visitors to the ranch played polo.

What is the name of Wyoming's first national parkway?

The John D. Rockefeller, Jr. Memorial Parkway was built between Yellowstone National Park and Grand Teton National Park. Established in 1972, the 23,000-acre monument is a tribute to the man who was responsible for the creation of a number of national parks.

Who was this country's first woman governor?

Nellie Tayloe Ross was elected governor in 1925 and served until 1927. (Her husband served as governor from 1923 until his death in 1924.) Mrs. Ross was then appointed by President Franklin Delano Roosevelt to head the U.S. Mint, a position she held until 1953.

Which Hollywood cowboy first worked as a wrangler on a Wyoming ranch as a young man?

Timothy John Fitzgerald McCoy, who starred in

early western films as Tim McCoy, was born in Michigan in 1891, and worked as a cowboy on a ranch in Thermopolis before he began his acting career in Hollywood. Some of the seventy films in which he starred were "Indians are Coming" in 1930, "Heroes of the Flames" in 1931, "Texas Cyclone" in 1932, "Silent Men" in 1933, "Hell Bent for Love" in 1934," "Square Shooter" in 1935, "Aces and Eights" in 1936, "Two Gun Justice" in 1938, "Texas Wildcats" in 1939, "Riders of Black Mountain" in 1940, "Forbidden Trails" in 1941, "West of the Law" in 1942, "Screen Snapshots out Hollywood Way," in 1953, "Around the World in 80 Days" in 1956, "Run of the Arrow" in 1960 and "Requiem of a Gunfighter" in 1965. McCoy appeared in twenty silent films before sound motion pictures were available. He also appeared in circus acts and produced his own short-lived "Tim McCoy Wild West Show" in 1938.

Which federal project was Wyoming's first?

A national historic engineering landmark, the Buffalo Bill Dam was originally known as the Shoshone Reservoir. Begun in 1899, the dam project was initiated by William F. Cody and his partner Nate Salisbury to provide for several thousand acres of farmland, but they ran out of money. The state of Wyoming later turned over the water rights to the federal government.

Where was the first business established in Wyoming?

Fur traders and mountain men, William Sublette and Robert Campbell, erected Fort William at the confluence of the North Platte and Laramie rivers in 1834. It was the first commercial enterprise west of the Missouri River. Sublette had earlier become a partner in the Rocky Mountain Fur Trading Company in 1826, purchased with three other trappers from William Ashley.

Who were the first women newspaper owners in the state?

Sisters Gertrude and Laura Huntington of Saratoga bought and operated the Platte Valley Lyre in 1890, and were known as the "Lyre Girls." Laura Huntington Heath served as the business manager and Gertrude as the Lyre's editor.

Where was the first Wyoming dude ranch?

The Eaton Ranch, located near Wolf, Wyoming, is eighteen miles west of Sheridan. The cattle and dude ranch encompasses 7,000 acres on the eastern slopes of the Big Horn Mountains. The term "dude" originated with the Eatons.

When did the bucking horse first appear on Wyoming license plates?

Allen T. True of Denver drew the bucking bronc

J. J. Hammond

in 1936 that has since adorned Wyoming license plates.

Prehistoric Wyoming

How old is the high plains land mass known as Wyoming?

The Rocky Mountain region was one of the first sections of molten earth to cool and solidify nearly four billion years ago.

Which prehistoric animals were most prevalent in the area?

Triceratops, Tyrannosaurus Rex, Brontosaurus, duck billed dinosaurs, and smaller reptiles as well as mammals were a few of the species that inhabited the wilderness. At least 250 species of Jurassic dinosaurs once roamed the area that is now Wyoming.

What produced the rock formations still visible in the Wyoming landscape?

Oceans washed across the land, leaving behind sandstones, limestone, shale, and the most ancient fish fossils to be found in this country. When the mountains were formed, anticlines and synclines developed, which contained petroleum and natural gas deposits.

Where did the ancient foraging people live?

The foragers lived in caves, grass wickiups, and beneath overhangs, using stone plates and mallets to grind seeds into meal.

Who were Wyoming's first artists?

Native Americans carved and etched their symbols and drawings in caves, overhangs, and stone. The petroglyphs and pictographs have been found in a great number of areas in the state. Petroglyphs are chiseled symbols, human and animal forms; pictographs are painted designs as well as drawings.

Who first inhabited the high plains area where prehistoric animals once roamed the region?

Nomadic tribes occupied the high plains more than 12,000 years ago, beginning with the Clovis people. They were followed by the Folsom Civilization about 2,000 years later. Prehistoric people inhabited Eden Valley 8,000 years ago and the first Paleo Indians hunted the hairy mammoth during the latter years of the Ice Age. Some of their projectile points have been found on Casper Mountain. Those who arrived after the Ice Age were gatherers rather than hunters, and survived on plants and small animals, gradually adapting to hunting larger mammals.

Where did the prehistoric foragers live following the Ice Age?

A prolonged drought followed the Ice Age, when most prehistoric people left the area now known as Wyoming. Those who remained retreated to the Mummy Caves near Cody where thirty-eight levels of civilization have been found, dating between 7000 and 2000 B.C.

What was the average life span for nomadic people?

The average nomad lived precariously for thirty-five to fifty years in small bands of twenty to one hundred people. When sand and grit wore down their teeth, they were unable to eat and died if they were not first killed by climatic conditions or animals.

How were bison and other large animals trapped for food and clothing?

The animals were herded over cliffs into sand traps. They were killed with spears and stone knives before the bow and arrow appeared on the high plains some 1,500 years ago. The oldest known animal kill site is located on the northwestern edge of Casper, Wyoming, near Interstate 25, and dates back to more than a thousand years.

What are the locations of the Wyoming dinosaur museums?

Dinosaur museums are located in Thermopolis, Laramie, Casper, and Glenrock. The University of Wyoming's Geological Museum conducts tours of its facility, which features skeletons of dinosaurs. They include Tyrannosaurus Rex, Allosaurus, Pteranodon, and Triceratops. The Casper College Tate Geological Museum has been listed in *Money Magazine* as one of the family friendliest dinosaur museums in the country. It has also been compared to the National Museum of Natural History at the Smithsonian Institute. Archeological digs are part of the museum's program. Another world class museum is the Wyoming Dinosaur Center and Dig Sites in Thermopolis, which features dioramas and life-sized dinosaur mounts as well as interpretive displays and exhibits. The museum houses over sixty dinosaur dig sites in a 500-acre area. Glenrock's paleontology museum focuses on "prehistoric life, including dinosaurs, ancient sea animals, Oligocene mammals, and modern animals."

The prehistoric stone quarries known

as the Spanish Diggings area are located where?

The diggings lie near the juncture of Niobrara, Goshen, and Platte counties north of Goshen, Wyoming, and southwest of Lusk. The 400 square mile location known as the Spanish Diggings contains the remains of prehistoric stone quarries where agate, quartzite, and jasper were mined. Evidence of the mining efforts has been found all over the western states. Early cowboys, who rode the eastern Wyoming range, believed the area was once a Spanish mine and referred to it as "the Spanish Diggings." Indians actually dug down with stone axes and primitive tools.

Where is Wyoming's medicine wheel?

The medicine wheel can be found 40 miles east of Lovell, Wyoming, at the summit of Medicine Mountain. The wheel contains 28 spokes and has a circumference of 245 feet. The ancient shrine was built of stone by a prehistoric tribe and is one of the state's unsolved mysteries.

Where was the first major discovery in the world of fossilized dinosaur bones?

An incredible amount of fossil dinosaur bones and Jurassic mammal bones were discovered in 1870 at Como Bluff, Wyoming, which is located halfway between Medicine Bow and Rock Creek. A Yale University paleontologist,

O.C. Marsh, arranged financing for the project and conducted most of the excavations, hence the name Marsh's dinosaurs. But violence erupted when Professor Edward Cope, a paleontologist from the Philadelphia Academy of Sciences, learned of the discovery and rushed to the excavation site. Both men hired excavation crews and fierce competition took place to locate the very best specimens. The stressful situation led to many possible acts of violence and the crews destroyed any bones left behind when they finished digging. The bone quarry was stripped bare of any important discoveries by the year 1889, and Marsh made lithographs from bones that were rejoined. The discovery of 250 known Jurassic North American mammals found in one small area is considered an archeological wonder.

Anthropologists speculate that humans have been present for 15,000 years in which region of Wyoming?

A number of anthropologists have speculated that continuous habitation occurred in the southeastern region of Wyoming for 15,000 years or more. Clovis projectile points, dating back 11,000 years, have been found in the Laramie and Casper areas. Evidence of habitation dating back 8,000 years has also been found in the Medicine Bow National Forest. The nomadic hunters depended upon large mammals for existence. A more temperate climate about

5,000 years ago resulted in the growth of short grasses, which prompted an influx of bison to the area.

Where is the building constructed from the oldest materials found on earth?

The fossil cabin in Como Butte, Wyoming, was built from the remains of dinosaur fossils excavated during the world's first discovery of more than 250 distinct species during the late 1800s. The structure still stands along the roadway and is a tourist attraction.

Wyoming's Native Americans

Which tribes have inhabited Wyoming?

The nomadic tribes included Arapaho, Arikara, Bannock, Blackfeet, Cheyenne, Crow, Gros Ventre, Kiowa, Nez Perce, Sheepeater, Sioux, Shoshone and the Utes. The Crow Indians and Shoshone were friendly to emigrants, but the Arapaho, Sioux, and Cheyenne created havoc along the Oregon Trail.

Which dialects have been spoken by the Arapaho nation and what have they traditionally called themselves?

Arapaho is a dialect of the Algonquin language and is still spoken by an estimated 1,000 people in Wyoming. The Gros Ventre dialect is also spoken by elderly natives and is currently being taught to younger members of the tribe. Arapahos have traditionally called themselves Inuna-Ina, ("our people") although they now refer to themselves as Arapaho. The Northern Arapaho are mainly concentrated in Wyoming, while the southern tribe lives in Oklahoma. Members of the Northern Arapaho tribe still speak the ancestral language.

Which two tribes were placed together on the Wind River Reservation despite hostilities between the two nations?

The Wind River Reservation was originally home to Chief Washakie's Shoshone tribe, beginning in 1860, but despite the antagonism between the two tribes, the Arapaho people were moved to the reservation in 1877. They repeatedly requested a separate reservation, but were denied.

Which Indian tribe allied itself with the U.S. Army?

The Shoshone people, led by Chief Washakie (1843-1900), were allied with the army, often serving as scouts. The Northern Arapaho, led by Chief Sharpnose, fought against the army and its Shoshone allies for an extended period, such as The Bates Battle, which took place in 1874 in current Hot Springs County, Wyoming.

Which national monument is known as the Mato Tipi or Bear's Lodge to Native

Americans?

Devil's Tower in northeastern Wyoming's Black Hills is considered a sacred site of great power to the Lakota, Tsistsistas, and other tribes of the Great Plains. Native Americans visit the site every year, particularly in June, to take part in spiritual rituals, including the Sun Dance which is observed near the time of the Summer Solstice

Chiefs Washakie and Sharpnose were two Native American leaders who ceded land to the government in 1896 for which state park?

The treaty of 1896 ceded the area of Hot Springs State Park to the U.S. government, which led to the establishment of the town of Thermopolis the next year. Chiefs Washakie and Sharpnose signed the treaty a year prior to Washakie's death.

Where is the largest collection in the nation of Indian artifacts, assembled by a single Wyoming family?

The Hot Springs County Museum's Native American collection includes many examples of Plains Indian beadwork as well as elk hide paintings, one of them created by Chief Washakie a month before his death. The Stephenson family's collection of arrowheads, spear points, scrapers, knives, awls, and beads consists of artifacts collected in south-central Wyoming over a 30-year period.

Which tribes took part in the attack on Platte Bridge Station on July 26, 1865?

An estimated 2,000 Sioux, Cheyenne, and Arapaho warriors took part in the attack, which resulted in the deaths of Eleventh Ohio Cavalry Lieutenant Caspar Collins and three of his men. All but three of Sergeant Amos Custard's Eleventh Kansas troopers, who were escorting the army supply wagons en route to the fort, were also killed. Later, two soldiers were killed when they tried to repair the telegraph line which had been cut down by the warriors to prevent communication between army posts in the area.

Which Cheyenne Chief was scalped and killed by the Platte Bridge soldiers in retaliation for their comrade's death?

On July 25, 1865, Cheyenne Chief High Back Wolf was scalped and killed by two young soldiers in the vicinity of Platte Bridge Station (later renamed Fort Caspar) in retaliation for the recent mutilation death of Private Bonwell, a soldier stationed at the fort. The incident occurred when Cheyenne warriors attempted to steal the army post's cattle herd. Captain Greer and thirty soldiers gave chase, Lieutenant Casper Collins among them.

Explorers and Mountain Men

Which Wyoming county was named in honor of a successful mountain man?

Sublette County took its name from William Sublette, who, with his partner Robert Campbell, built Fort William, which was later renamed Fort Laramie. Born in Kentucky in 1799, Sublette died in Pennsylvania in 1845.

When did French fur trapping begin?

Although the British Hudson's Bay Company in 1670 began trading goods for animal pelts in North America, it wasn't until the mid-1700s that French maps show fur trapping activities took place. Evidence of some earlier Spanish explorers has been unearthed; however, the Wyoming wilderness remained uninhabited by white emigrants until John Colter explored Yellowstone in 1807, and members of the Astor fur trading party arrived in 1812. There were subsequent visits by explorers and mountain men during the 1820s.

Who left Lewis and Clark's expedition to explore and trap in the area now known as Yellowstone Park and Wyoming's Absaroka Mountain in 1806?

John Colter is credited with being the first white man to explore what is now known as Yellowstone National Park. His descriptions of the geysers and other geothermal phenomena were later known as "Colter's Hell." Colter is said to have been revered by fellow trappers, traders, and mountain men alike.

Which mountain man, born in southern New York in 1799, carried a bible with him on his travels, and refused to swear, drink alcohol, or chew tobacco?

Jedediah Smith not only carried his bible with him, he also took copies of Lewis and Clark's journals on his travels. Smith led a group of men south of the Yellowstone to open up new trapping grounds, and rediscovered the Rocky Mountains' South Pass. Later, badly mauled by a bear, the mountain man suffered a serious scalp wound. When he returned to St. Louis in 1825 with 9,000 pounds of beaver skins, he combed his hair forward to disguise his scars, a practice he continued for the rest of his life. The most traveled mountain man was killed in 1831 by Comanche warriors along the Santa Fe Trail. He was 32. His gravesite monument, located at Old Town in Cody, Wyoming, is pictured on the front cover of this book.

Who was the first to hold rendezvous for the purpose of trading goods for furs?

William Ashley began the practice in 1825. A competitor, the American Fur Company, also established trading posts along the Upper Missouri River, one of them called Fort Union. Mountain men-traders, Campbell and Sublette, constructed their own trading station less than three miles from Fort Union.

Where and when were the rendezvous held?

Mountain men fur trading "conventions" were held to share information about the fur trade as well as buy supplies to sustain them for another year in the Rocky Mountain region. The first mountain rendezvous was held in 1825 at Henry's Fork on the Green River in Wyoming. It was followed by the camp in Cache Valley in 1826; Bear Lake in 1827 and 1828; Pierre's Hole in 1829; Popo Agie in 1830; Cache Valley in 1831; Pierre's Hole in 1832; Green River in 1833; the tributary on the Green River in 1834; Green River in 1835, 1836, and 1837; Popo Agie in 1838; Green River in 1839; and Horse Creek in 1840.

J. J. Hammond

Who answered William Ashley's help wanted ad in the *Missouri Gazette* and *Public Advisor* in 1822?

Some seventy young men responded to the ad for fur trappers. Among those who agreed to join Ashley's party were William Sublette, Jedediah Smith, Hugh Glass, Tom Fitzpatrick, David Jackson, James Beckwourth and Jim Bridger. Sublette traveled to the Northwest, where he formed a partnership with Smith and David Jackson. Later, they purchased Ashley's Rocky Mountain Fur Trading Company, and Sublette and Smith were briefly involved in the Santa Fe trade, but Sublette returned to the Rocky Mountains following Jedediah Smith's death. Sublette had been wounded at the Battle of Pierre's Hole during July of 1832. When he recovered, he established a new company with Robert Campbell, which they later sold to the American Fur Trading Company.

Who was Thomas Fitzpatrick?

Tom Fitzpatrick joined William Ashley's fur trading party in 1822 with fellow trappers Hugh Glass, Jim Bridger, Jedediah Smith, Jim Beckwourth, William Sublette and William Jackson. William Ashley's party of seventy men were attacked by Arikaras and twelve of them were killed. Fitzpatrick survived to buy the Rocky Mountain Fur Company in 1830 with four partners. The Irishman headed the company and again escaped with his life in 1832 during the Battle of Pierre's Hole. Known as "White Hair" and "Broken Hand," he sold the company in 1841 and became a guide for such men as John C. Fremont, Father DeSmet, John Bidwell, and Stephen Kearney.

Which priest christened Independence Rock "The Great Register of the Desert?"

Jean Pierre DeSmet, a Belgian Jesuit Priest and missionary among the Indians, christened the huge monolith in 1840. He was preceded by Captain Bonneville in 1832 and travelers as early as 1813. Father DeSmet, for whom a northern Wyoming lake was named, carved his initials in the gargantuan boulder along with a large cross. He covered the cross with India rubber to protect it from the elements.

Which fur traders built the first dwelling in what is now Natrona County?

A member of the Astor fur trading party, Robert Stuart led a party of six men east on the route that later became known as the Oregon Trail. They built a primitive cabin in what is now Natrona County, but abandoned it after a few weeks in 1812 when they learned that a band of Arapaho were camped in the area.

Which former Indian fighter returned to the Rockies to live with the Shoshones and teach them to farm?

Frontiersman "Finn" Burnett lived with the Shoshones and he taught them agricultural techniques. As a civilian Indian fighter, he had accompanied General Crook on his expedition to force the Sioux onto reservations, and took part in the June 17, 1876 Rosebud Creek Battle in Montana against Crazy Horse eight days before the Battle of the Little Big Horn. Among his descendants were former governor and U.S. senator, Milward Simpson and his sons: Alan and Peter.

Which explorer led the first western winter charting expedition (at the age of 29) as well as in 1849, where, in the San Juan Mountains, many of his men died?

John C. Fremont, who traveled extensively with Kit Carson as his guide, was responsible for both expeditions, the latter resulting in the deaths of a number of his men, who froze to death in the San Juan Mountains.

Which African American trapper was a Crow war chief?

Jim Beckwourth (1798-1866) was not only a mountain man-trader, he was a war chief of the Crow Indian tribe. While in the gold fields of California, he dictated his life story to Thomas D. Bonner, an itinerant justice of the peace. Published as *The Life and Adventures of James P. Beckwourth, Mountaineer, Scout, Pioneer,* and *Chief of the Crow Nation of Indians* was produced by Harper and brothers in 1856. The book was also published in England that year and in France in 1870. His contemporaries considered Beckwourth's accounts as highly exaggerated.

Which trading items were the most heavily stocked at the 1825 Rendezvous on Henry's Fork of the Green River?

William Ashley stocked one thousand flints, 200 pounds of coffee, two and a half kegs of tobacco, and 130 pounds of sugar, which were preferred items for sale or trade, according to his diary. Other necessities included horseshoes, beads, knives, blue stroud cloth, beaver skins, gun powder, lead bars, axes, hoes, and a variety of Indian trinkets and ribbons.

Which explorer/trapper led the first crossing of the Rocky Mountains with an expedition and twenty supply wagons?

Born in France, April 13, 1796, Benjamin Louis de Bonneville arrived with his family in this country in 1803. Bonneville received a degree in engineering from West Point and requested a leave of absence to lead a geographical and mill data expedition to the West Coast. Bonneville was asked by government officials to gather intelligence on western geography, Indian tribes, and the British presence in the continental Northwest. The government, according to the California Military Museum, was "unable, or unwilling to support exploratory and intelligence gathering missions financially, and depended upon 'spies' like Lieutenant Zebulon Pike, John C. Fremont, and Captain Benjamin Bonneville" to deliver intelligence reports. Captain Bonneville and 110 men left Missouri on May 1, 1832, on a "fur trapping expedition," and returned more than four years later, so late that he was considered AWOL, but Bonneville had provided the government with valuable information about the western terrain, Indian warfare, and British occupation of the Northwest. His party attempted to establish a way station near South Pass, Wyoming, but a heavy accumulation of snow discouraged the attempt. While visiting Independence Rock, the captain and his men carved their names and initials in the monolith. Utah's Bonneville Salt Flats was later named in his honor, although the explorer had never been there.

Which well known artist was present at the 1837 Green River Rendezvous?

Alfred Jacob Miller was the only artist to paint and sketch rendezvous participants. Hired by Captain William Drummond Stuart, he traveled with members of the American Fur Company caravan.

Which fur trapper traveled to the Rocky

Mountains for his health?

Colonel Robert Campbell, who later became William Sublette's partner, was advised by his doctor to travel to the Rockies to cure his consumption. A pale young man subject to lung hemorrhages, Campbell trapped, operated fur trading posts from 1825-1835, and survived the Battle of Pierre's Hole. During 1851 Campbell attended the 18-day Grand Council of Sioux, Crows, Blackfeet, and Cheyenne at the mouth of Horse Creek on the North Platte River. He also accompanied Father DeSmet to Fort Laramie the following year to attend the Plains Indian Treaty Council and dictated his adventures to William Fayel in 1870.

How did Captain Bonneville distinguish between American and French trappers?

The author, Washington Irving, bought the rights to Bonneville's journal and quoted the captain in his book, *The Adventures of Captain Bonneville*. The explorer-trapper wrote: "The American mountain man stands by himself, and is peerless for the service of the wilderness. Drop him in the midst of a prairie, or in the heart of the mountains, and he is never at a loss. He notices every landmark; can retrace his route through the most monotonous plains, or most perplexed labyrinths of the mountains; no danger nor difficulty can appall him, and he scorns to complain under any privation."

Of the French or Creole, Bonneville said, "The French trapper is represented as a lighter, softer, more self-indulgent kind of man. He must have his Indian wife, his lodge, and his petty conveniences. He is gay and thoughtless, takes little heed of landmarks, depends upon his leaders and companions to think for the common weal, and, if left to himself, is easily perplexed and lost."

Which mountain man-trapper was the first to measure the Bozeman Trail?

Jim Bridger (1804-1881), guided the Powder River Expedition and was the first to measure the length of the Bozeman Trail from Fort Laramie, Wyoming, to Virginia City, Montana, in 1865, a distance of roughly 600 miles. Bridger built a trading post in southwestern Wyoming, when the fur trade diminished, to provide supplies to emigrants traveling the Oregon Trail. Bridger is said to have been the first white man to discover the Great Salt Lake and one of the first to explore what is now Yellowstone Park and South Pass. A guide for explorers and Indian fighters, he also led U.S. troops into Utah during the Mormon War of 1857-1858.

Who was Christopher Houston Carson?

Christopher Houston "Kit" Carson (1809-1868) was only nine when his father was killed in Missouri. Kit was the ninth child of a family of fourteen when he was apprenticed to a saddle maker at age 14, but soon left for the Southwest where he was a cook and harness repairman. At 19, Carson joined a fur trapping expedition to California and eventually arrived in the Rocky Mountains, where he married the first of his two Indian wives, an Arapaho and Cheyenne. A man of small stature, Carson was known for his honesty and courage. While in Missouri, where he enrolled his daughter in a convent following her mother's death, he met John C. Fremont and became his guide for Fremont's first mapping expedition in the West in 1842. He continued as Fremont's guide until 1846, just prior to the Mexican-American War. Fremont's widely read reports about his mapping expeditions made Kit Carson a national hero.

Which mountain man swore to kill Jim Bridger and John Fitzpatrick because they left him to die?

Born in Ireland at the turn of the nineteenth century, Hugh Glass immigrated at a young age with his parents to this country. He answered William Ashley's ad in the *Missouri Gazette* and *Public Adviser* in 1822 and was one of the first to travel to the Rockies to take part in fur trapping. Glass was known for his bravery, and survived wounds at the hands of the Arikara as well as a near fatal bear mauling. Andrew Henry, leader of the fur trading party, left Jim Bridger and John Fitzgerald to take care of Glass, but believing that he was dying, the two men abandoned him and took his gun and trapping equipment. They then reported to Henry that Glass had died. The trapper managed to crawl to the Grand River where Indians helped him recover from his injuries. Once he recovered, he was determined to kill the men who abandoned him, but changed his mind when he located Bridger and learned that Fitzgerald had left the area to join the army. Glass was killed by Indians in 1833 along the Yellowstone River.

Forts and Battlefields

Which Wyoming Fort was constructed to protect the overland mail service in southern Wyoming?

Originally established as a fur trading outpost, the fort built by William Sublette and his partner Robert Campbell in 1834 was sold to the military to protect the Overland Mail Service and emigrant travelers. Renamed Fort Laramie, the post was located in southeastern Wyoming, and situated along the Oregon and Mormon trails. The fort was also located near the Texas cattle trail as well as the Deadwood Stage Route. Fort Laramie was officially closed in 1890.

Who was involved in the Battle of Red Buttes?

The battle took place within sight of Platte Bridge Station. On July 26, 1865, Sgt. Amos Custard and his army supply wagons approached the fort from Sweetwater Station and were attacked by an estimated 2,000 warriors. Lt. Caspar Collins led a patrol of twenty men to escort Custard's supply train, but he and three of his men were killed as well as all but three of Custard's 11th Kansas troopers. The remaining soldiers raced to the fort and survived with the help of other troopers. The fort and city of Casper were later named for Lieutenant Caspar Collins, but the city's name was misspelled by a recording clerk.

Why was Fort Caspar established?

The fort was built in 1862 to protect the transcontinental telegraph line, Overland Mail Service, and the emigrants traveling the Oregon, Mormon, and California trails. Originally called Platte Bridge Station, the post was renamed Fort Caspar in 1865.

What prompted the attacks on Wyoming forts by Red Cloud and other Indian strategists?

The Sand Creek Massacre of November 29, 1864, is still considered the most grievous assault on plains Indians by the natives, themselves. A group of 700 soldiers led by Colonel John M. Chivington attacked a village of Southern Cheyenne and Arapaho along Sand Creek in Colorado Territory, slaughtering an estimated 150 Indians. The attack so inflamed Ogallala Chief Red Cloud and other plains Indians that they waged war on army forts and civilian installations. Red Cloud was also enraged when he learned that the government had already begun building forts along the Bozeman Trail before he had signed the non-aggression treaty for plains Indians at Fort Laramie. He reportedly stormed out of the fort, threatening everyone within earshot to hold on to their scalps.

Which army post survived the Fort Laramie treaty of 1869?

Fort Fetterman was built in 1867 on the bluffs overlooking the North Platte River near present Douglas, Wyoming. Because of its location, the fort was excluded from the provisions of the Treaty of Fort Laramie, which provided for the abandonment of all forts located north of the Platte. Fetterman was therefore the northern most fort established in eastern Wyoming. The army abandoned the post in 1882.

Which army fort was built to protect the emigrants traveling the Bozeman Trail to the gold fields in Montana?

Fort Phil Kearny was established in 1866 by Colonel Henry Carrington of the 18th Infantry near the present northeastern Wyoming town of Story. The fort, named for a popular Union general, was the largest of three forts, which included Fort Reno near Kaycee, Wyoming, and C. F. Smith near Hardin, Montana. The army posts were built not only to protect emigrants traveling the Bozeman Trail and crews building the transcontinental railroad south of the fort, they were designed to prevent intertribal warfare. The fort existed two years before it was abandoned and burned by Indian warriors.

Who was responsible for the Fetterman Massacre?

Capt. William J. Fetterman disregarded orders on December 21, 1866, and led his party of eighty men in pursuit of Sioux warriors from the area of Fort Phil Kearny woodcutting detail. They were led into ambush by a superior force of Indians, and all the soldiers were killed in what has become known as the Fetterman Massacre.

What precipitated the Wagon Box Fight?

Captain Powell and his company of soldiers from Fort Phil Kearny were riding patrol in the foothills of the Big Horn Mountains to guard the civilian woodcutting crew on August 2, 1867, when they were attacked by an estimated 1,500 Lakota Sioux led by Red Cloud and Crazy Horse. Those who could escape, rode for the fort, while the others, Powell included, sought shelter behind a circle of wagon boxes in an open field. Three or four men were killed, but the 32 soldiers fought waves of warriors with their newly issued .50 caliber Springfield breech loading rifles, holding the natives at bay until reinforcements arrived from Fort Phil Kearny.

Who was John "Portuguese" Phillips and why was a monument erected in his honor?

A monument stands near Fort Phil Kearny in honor of John "Portuguese" Phillips, who carried the news of the Fetterman massacre through 236 miles of hostile Indian country during late December of 1866, from Fort Phil Kearny to Fort Laramie. Born in the Azore Islands, Phillips became a folk hero in the cowboy state following his dangerous ride.

Which early Wyoming fort later became the site of Warren Air Force Base in Cheyenne?

Fort Russell was named for Brevet Major General David Alan Russell, a union army officer during the Civil War. The fort was established in 1867 near Crow Crossing, later renamed Cheyenne, to protect the construction crews from the Indians while they built the transcontinental railroad. The fort, located midway in the country, served as a military supply station, and was, at one point, cavalry headquarters for the army.

Which fort was named for the colonel who defeated Dull Knife's band?

Fort Mackenzie was named for Ranald Slide Mackenzie, a Civil War veteran and colonel of the Fourth Cavalry, who took part in the Powder River Expedition of 1876. Mackenzie led a mounted column of soldiers during General George Crook's winter campaign and surprised and defeated Chief Dull Knife's band of northern Cheyenne. Fort Mackenzie was established in the Sheridan area in 1898 to protect settlers in the Rocky Mountain region, although fighting had ceased and Indians had been relocated on reservations twenty years earlier. The garrison reached its peak in 1911 with 601 men. Fort Mackenzie was officially abandoned in 1918. Four years later the fort was converted to a Veteran's Administration hospital and remains so to this day.

Which fort was first built along the Bozeman Trail?

Built during the spring of 1865, the permanent fort was established on the Powder River near the Bozeman Trail crossing in the Kaycee area to punish Sioux and Cheyenne warriors for their attacks along the Platte River. First called Fort Connor, it was renamed Fort Reno a few months later. Few battles occurred, however, and the fort was abandoned during the fall of 1868 after Fort Phil Kearny was built sixty miles to the north.

When was Fort Yellowstone established?

The fort was established in 1886 to protect the national park from poachers, souvenir hunters, and anyone who would damage the land and its natural wonders. The fort was also constructed because of mismanagement by the previous civilian superintendents. Soldiers of Company M, First U.S. Cavalry of Fort Custer, Montana, arrived to provide more than thirty years of military protection for Yellowstone Park. The company, led by Capt. Moses Harris, lived at Camp Sheridan and was located at Mammoth Hot Springs Terraces, but harsh weather forced Congress to appropriate $50,000 to build a permanent post named Fort Yellowstone.

Where was Fort Fred Steele built?

Established in 1868, Fort Fred Steele was occupied for the next twenty years. Built to protect the transcontinental railroad from Indian attacks in southern Wyoming. It was located on the west bank of the North Platte River. The post was named for a Civil War hero, Major General Frederick Steele of the 20th U.S. Infantry. As many as 300 troops were stationed at the fort that was originally a tent city.

Whose attack on the village of Chief Black Bear prompted Indian survivors to align themselves with the Sioux and Cheyenne warriors?

General Patrick E. Connor, commander of the Powder River Expedition, led troops in an attack on a generally peaceful Arapaho village during August 1865. Women and children were among those killed, and the tribe's winter food supplies and tipis were destroyed. Surviving Arapahos later joined forces with Sioux and Cheyenne warriors to retaliate by attacking Col. James A. Sawyer's road surveying expedition that year in the Ranchester, Wyoming, area. They attacked Fort Phil Kearny the following year and took part in the Wagon Box Fight in 1867.

When was Fort Bridger established?

Fort Bridger was a trading post jointly owned by the mountain man-trapper, Jim Bridger, and his partner, Louis Vasquez. Located on Black's Fork in southwestern Wyoming, the post was built in 1843 to cater to emigrants. The original buildings were burned in 1857 during the Mormon War. The following year, Albert Sidney Johnson assumed command of the fort on behalf of the Mormon Church.

Wyoming Outlaws

Who were the most infamous of outlaws to inhabit the Hole in the Wall hideout?

Robert Leroy Parker, alias Butch Cassidy, and his Wild Bunch gang are credited with making the Hole in the Wall outlaw hideout famous. Among Cassidy's cohorts were Elzy Lay, Harry "Sundance Kid" Longabaugh, Harvey "Kid Curry" Logan, Ben "The Tall Texan" Kilpatrick, and William Carver. Hundreds of other lesser known outlaws also inhabited the area on a temporary basis.

Who were the first known lawbreakers to inhabit the Hole in the Wall's outlaw cave?

Civil War deserters are known to have hidden in the cave during the 1860s, as did Jesse and Frank James following their train robbery in Carbon

County, Wyoming, in 1878. Other temporary cave dwellers were "Big Nose" George Parrott's Powder River Gang from 1874 until 1881. The outlaw cave is located on the Middle Fork of the Powder River.

Which former Pinkerton Detective was hanged as an outlaw in Cheyenne in 1903?

Tom Horn was hanged for the killing of Willie Nickel, a 14-year old boy who was reportedly mistaken for his suspected rustler father in the predawn hours. There is doubt that Horn actually committed the murder but Marshal Joe LeFors extracted a confession from Horn by plying him with liquor in his jail cell.

Which bungling horse thief caused the Wild Bunch gang to botch the Belle Fourche, South Dakota, bank robbery in 1897?

Tom "Peep" O'Day, an inept, alcoholic horse thief, was briefly a member of the Wild Bunch. He was booted out of the gang when he spent too much time in a local saloon instead of reconnoitering the Belle Fourche bank. O'Day was arrested following the robbery when his horse bolted and followed the other bank robbers out of town. He was acquitted of the bank robbery charges but was later arrested by Natrona County Sheriff Webb for horse theft, and spent some time in the Wyoming Penitentiary.

Which member of the Wild Bunch was well read and a literary society member at the age of 14?

Harry Longabaugh, alias the Sundance Kid, was a teenage member of his hometown literary society. He was born in Mont Clare, Pennsylvania, in 1867, and jailed in Sundance, Wyoming, for the theft of a horse and saddle when he was 18. He then took the town's name when he rode the outlaw trail.

Which two Wyoming border towns were frequented by members of the Wild Bunch and other outlaws?

Baggs and Dixon, small towns on the Colorado border, were often visited by the outlaws when they left Brown's Hole. The isolated area in southern Carbon County, Wyoming, was an occasional haven for the Wild Bunch. Butch Cassidy's gang stayed in Baggs at the Vernon Hotel, where they shot up the Bulldog Saloon and paid the owner a dollar for each of 25 bullet holes.

Where did the "outlaw trail" begin and end?

The trail began across the Canadian border in "Big Muddy." It then entered northeastern Montana and looped into mid-western North Dakota, exiting through the northwestern corner of South Dakota before entering the northeastern corner of Wyoming and running diagonally across the state through the Hole in the Wall. The trail lead southwest to Brown's Hole in the northwestern border of Colorado, and into Robbers Roost in eastern Utah. The trail then looped back eastward into southwestern Colorado and led to northeastern Arizona and Alma, New Mexico. Outlaws rode southeastward from Alma into Ciudad Juarez, Mexico, where the trail usually ended.

Which outlaw earned his nickname from a kick by a horse?

"Flat Nose" George Currie (Curry), a cattle rustler turned bank and train robber, was a member of Butch Cassidy's Wild Bunch for several years. He took part in the botched Belle Fourche bank robbery and was later killed near Thompson, Utah, by lawmen after he returned to his cattle rustling trade. George Currie earned his nickname after a horse kicked his face, flattening the bridge of his nose.

Which outlaw and his brothers adopted George Currie's surname when they rode with the Wild Bunch?

George Currie was Harve(y) Logan's mentor when the young man fled to the Hole in the Wall after shooting Pike Landusky in the town of the same name in Montana, (although his antagonist misfired first.) Logan reportedly became known as "Kid Curry" and his younger brothers, Johnny and "Lonie," also took the last name as aliases. "Kid Curry" became a member of Butch Cassidy's Wild Bunch and was said to have been the meanest and deadliest outlaw to roam the West.

Which outlaw was known as George Parrott because of the size of his nose?

George Manuse, known as "Big Nose" George Parrott, (sometimes confused with "Flat Nose" George Curry), attempted to rob a Union Pacific train with "Dutch" Charley Clark and two accomplices. In 1878 Parrott tried to derail the train near Medicine Bow, but a railroad worker noticed the misalignment of tracks and notified authorities. Parrott and Clark were later taken into custody separately. Angry citizens hanged Clark from a telephone pole in 1879, and Parrott when he was apprehended in 1881. A young Rawlins doctor, J.E. Osbourne, cut off the top of the outlaw's skull and sent Parrott's skin to a Denver tannery to have shoes and a medical bag made from them. The doctor, who became Wyoming governor (1893-1895), is said to have worn the shoes while holding office as well as on special occasions. George Parrott's shoes and skull are currently on display at the Carbon County Museum.

Which red-haired bandit warned the Union Pacific Railroad before he held up passenger trains?

William "Bill" Carlisle's first known robbery was committed in 1916 when he robbed the Union Pacific train by holding his gun on the brakeman and forcing him to collect money from the male passengers. Because train robbery was a state capital offense, the crime drew national attention and a $1,000 reward was offered by the railroad. Union Pacific officials received a note from Carlisle a few weeks later, warning that he planned to conduct another train robbery. Although the railroad hired detectives to ride the trains, Carlisle hopped aboard in Cheyenne, and repeated his earlier robbery. He then jumped from the train and walked to Casper, buying food at ranches along the way. The likeable bandit again notified the railroad of an intended robbery, which he carried out by robbing the men and jumping from the train. He was captured several days later and served three years and five months in the Wyoming penitentiary before he escaped and robbed another train between Rock River and Medicine Bow. Shot in the hand while escaping, Carlisle was again shot and captured at a remote ranch in Converse County. When he recovered, he was returned to prison where he spent his time reading law books. He reportedly became a model prisoner.

Where was the Hole in the Wall Bar located?

Tom Skinner's Hole-in-the-Wall Bar was located

in Thermopolis, a favorite hangout of Butch Cassidy's Wild Bunch, where they had many friends. The saloon was demolished during the 1970s but the cherry wood bar was purchased by the Pioneer Association and moved to the Hot Springs County Museum in Thermopolis.

Homesteading

What did the Preemption Act of 1841 allow U.S. citizens to do?

Congress passed the 1841 Preemption Act to allow U.S. citizens to squat on government land and buy up to 160 acres. The virgin land's selling price was $1.25 an acre; however, the first homestead patent wasn't issued in Wyoming for thirty years. The majority of land seekers during that period were interested in cattle grazing, not farming, and 160 acres would only support a herd of five or six cattle.

What were the 1862 Homestead Act requirements?

When the Homestead Act was passed by Congress in 1862, following more than seventy years of controversy over the distribution of public lands, the Free Soil Party demanded that free land ownership become a means of stopping the spread of slavery into the territories. The demand was adapted into the 1860 Republican platform, which prompted the southern states to secede from the union. The measure was then adopted. The act that became law in 1863 cleared the way for any citizen to file on a quarter-section (160 acres) of land to own in five years if a house were built, a well excavated, the land fenced, and at least ten acres tilled under.

Which subsequent laws allowed stock growers to file on up to 1,120 acres of land?

The 1862 Homestead Act was followed by the 1873 Timber Culture Act and the Desert Land Act of 1877. The combined 1,120 acres were still not enough to support a herd of more than 38 head of cattle because each cow required at least 30 acres of Wyoming land on which to survive. The railroad sold much of its land to cattlemen, who, when additional land was needed, paid their employees to homestead land and turn it over once it had been "proved up" on.

When was the Dry Land Act enacted?

The 1909 Dry Land Act was passed to encourage emigration to Wyoming, but a severe drought the following year caused crop failures, which lasted for the next two years. By 1913 bumper crops were experienced in various areas of the state. Farming in many areas at that time, however, created tragic experiences and most farmers in the central plains were eventually forced to sell or relinquish their land and move into town.

When was the Wind River Reservation land lottery held?

The land lottery was held in 1906 following a 1904 meeting between government officials and tribal leaders to discuss settlement of surplus reservation land. The land opening resulted in individual farming operations under the Homestead Act near the bend of the Wind River as well as the town of Riverton, Wyoming. The income from the lottery helped to ease years of poverty suffered by the Shoshone and Arapaho tribes by paying tribal members on a per capita basis and providing for educational facilities and irrigation systems.

What caused homesteaders to give up on their allotted Wind River lands?

Wind River homesteaders were hampered by the delays in promised canal construction for much needed irrigation water. Construction of canals proved to be more difficult than government officials anticipated, so the Bureau of Reclamation took over the project during the 1920s and new homestead lands were opened up as the canals were built. Homesteading continued into the 1950s. For some farmers with insufficient water to irrigate their crops, commuting into Riverton to hold down jobs became a matter of survival. Other central Wyoming farmers gave up and left their land, which they had acquired under the 1916 Grazing Act. After years of marginal living on dry land farms that were only fit for stock grazing (although 640 acres was not enough to sustain a profitable herd), the most stubborn commuted by train to Casper, or to the soda lakes in Sweetwater Valley while trying to hold onto their land. Others valiantly held title to their land when oil was discovered in central Wyoming, hoping that someone would drill on their property.

When was the Homestead Act repealed?

The Homestead Act remained in effect until 1977, the year it was repealed. Because many homesteaders sold their land once they had "proved up" on it, most of the more desirable allotments were under the control of the railroads and land speculators. Settlers were then forced to buy from speculators rather than accept inferior government land. By the turn of the twentieth century, some 600,000 farmers had fulfilled the necessary requirements to own 80,000 million acres of homestead lands.

Cattle and the Cattle Wars

Who brought the first small cattle herd to Wyoming?

The Sublette brothers brought five head of cattle to Wyoming Territory in 1830 for the Wind River Rendezvous. They were followed by thousands of bovine travelers accompanying wagon trains.

What caused the Johnson County War?

Cattlemen, frustrated by the increase in rustling and the courts inability to convict those who were caught, took the law into their own hands by invading Johnson County, Wyoming, with Texas mercenaries in 1892. The fifty-two men ambushed and killed suspected rustlers Nate Champion and Nick Ray, and were rescued from angry citizens by the National Guard before they could be blown up with their own dynamite at the TA Ranch near Buffalo.

J. J. Hammond

When was the peak year of cattle drives?

The peak year of cattle drives was 1884, when approximately 300 herds with 800,000 head of cattle left Texas for the northwest. About 400 cowhands and 30,000 horses accompanied the cattle in an unprecedented bovine relocation.

Why was Wyoming Territory considered one of the best open ranges to graze cattle?

Cattle lost from wagon trains were discovered along the California-Oregon trails that had wintered well in Wyoming Territory. The area soon became known as one of the best short-grass, open ranges in the country.

Where did cattle originate that were trailed to Wyoming?

Long-horned cattle were driven up from Texas on the Chisholm, Western, and Goodnight Loving Trails. Herefords were shipped from the British Isles and cattle poured into the territory from the Midwest until 1885, when Wyoming rangeland was overstocked with an estimated two million head, valued at nearly $100 million.

How did dishonest cattle promoters bilk easterner investors out of hundreds of thousands of dollars?

Con men sold worthless stock in nonexistent Wyoming cattle herds. Cattle dealers also took advantage of wealthy men such as English financier Sir Moreton Frewen. During the early 1880s, Frewen was sold the same herd twice by con men who herded the same cattle around a hill a second time.

What caused the cattle growing bonanza to fail?

The severely cold winter of 1886-1887, coupled with declining cattle prices, brought stockmen to the verge of panic. Steers that had previously sold for $54 in 1884 were only bringing $46 the following year. The Scottish-owned Swan Land and Cattle Company failure in 1887 sent shock waves throughout the stock growing community and the bottom fell out of the business for foreign investors.

Which homesteaders were hanged so that a cattleman could take over their property?

Homesteaders were routinely harassed and driven from their land, but the hangings of James and Ellen Watson-Averell were among the most infamous crimes of Wyoming's nineteenth century. "Ella" Watson-Averell became known as "Cattle Kate" upon her death, when cattlemen spread rumors that she had received stolen calves in exchange for her favors. Her homesteaded land, along with that of her husband, was later purchased by A.J. Bothwell, one of the cattlemen responsible for the hangings.

Who were the cattlemen responsible for the Averell hangings?

Prominent Sweetwater Valley cattlemen, Albert Bothwell, R.M. Gailbraith, Tom Sun, Robert Connor, John Durbin, and dairyman Earnest McClain took part in the kidnappings and hangings of the Averell couple. Although the cattlemen were brought to trial, witnesses disappeared and the men were set free.

How did outlaws rebrand stolen cattle?

Outlaws such as Butch Cassidy's Wild Bunch sold rustled cattle to construction crews who laid railroad tracks across Montana. The brands that could not be altered were cut from the cattle and replaced with branded patches of hide which were sewn on with needle and thread. New brand inspection laws, however, put an end to the practice.

Where were rustled cattle grazed to fatten, brand, and butcher before selling them to the railroad crews in Montana?

The infamous Hole in the Wall canyon in central Wyoming was the site of many herds of rustled cattle. During the spring thaw, area ranchers would find large bundles of cowhides weighted with rocks and bailing wire that had floated out of the Hole in the Wall canyon along Upper Buffalo Creek. The butchered beef was sold to the Union Pacific and Baltimore and

Ohio construction camps by the outlaws until branding laws were enacted.

Which brand inspector accompanied a cowboy army into the Hole in the Wall to retrieve stolen cattle?

Marshal Joe LeFors dedicated his career to capturing Butch Cassidy's Wild Bunch, but he never quite succeeded. Cassidy instigated the large scale rustling operation in the Hole in the Wall and LeFors accompanied a cowboy army there to retrieve stolen cattle after they had been abandoned by the outlaws.

What further frustrated cattlemen in their attempts to hold onto the Wyoming Territory rangelands?

Sheep were first trailed in from New Mexico by the Durbin brothers and their partner, C.W. Rinter during the early 1870s. The flocks were later increased by 1,500 Oregon wethers. Other ranchers soon followed suit. Cattlemen claimed that sheep trampled vegetation and ate grass to the roots, ruining the rangeland for cattle. Range wars erupted and many sheep and their herders were killed.

Ghost Towns

Why was South Pass City established?

Gold was discovered in southwestern Wyoming by an American Fur Company trapper in 1842, but the general public was unaware of the find until 1867 when the Carissa Mine was opened and the town of South Pass City was established. The subsequent gold rush resulted in stage service, a newspaper, bank, and designation as the Carter County seat. The name was later changed to Sweetwater County and a toll road was built to Atlantic City, a distance of two and a half miles.

Which town claimed to have established the state's first brewery?

Atlantic City, founded in 1868, claimed to have housed Wyoming Territory's first brewery. The mining town was known for its French quarter, which catered to miners. After the gold began to diminish, the town lost most of its estimated 360 residents. A later mining attempt by a Frenchman, Emil Granier, failed and the town shrank to a handful of residents.

Which southwestern town literally died from a lack of water?

The town of Bryan in southwestern Wyoming was founded in 1868 with the expectation that it would become a transportation center. A roundhouse was built as well as a bank, large hotel, and stage service station. Because of a lack of water, the Union Pacific decided to move the roundhouse to Green River City, and all that remains of the isolated town is a few crumbling foundations.

Which oilfield town near Salt Creek was named for an area homesteader?

The short-lived boomtown of Lavoye was named for homesteader Louis Lavoye. Money briefly flowed like oilfield gushers during the early 1920s, when fortunes were won and lost overnight. After surviving a serious typhoid epidemic and disastrous fire in 1925, residents abandoned their squatter's rights to land leases by the Ohio Oil Company. They moved their town a few miles north to a new location on the edge of the Salt Creek Oilfield. A few crumbled remains of buildings are still in evidence in northeastern Natrona County.

Which stagecoach station was built in the vicinity of Rock Springs, to transport passengers to South Pass City?

Point of Rocks Stage Station, twenty-two miles northeast of Rock Springs was built in 1862 by Ben Holladay after Indian raids prevented stage traffic along the Oregon Trail. The station was burned by the Indians, but not before the stage line's former superintendent, Jack Slade, held up the stage and killed seven passengers in 1863.

Which neighboring Atlantic City town was originally named Hamilton City.

Miners Delight, once called Hamilton City, was located less than three miles from Atlantic City, when the Miners Delight Mine was discovered in 1867. The town was abandoned in 1907 after the gold supply diminished.

Where was the current ghost town of Bald Mountain City established?

Fine grained gold was discovered in Sheridan County, Wyoming, in 1890, prompting an influx of prospectors to the area for ten years in the vicinity of the Little Horn River and Porcupine Creek. The Fortunatas Mining and Milling Company bought a number of claims and the town of Bald Mountain City was established. All that remains of the town, which lies to the east of the Medicine Wheel National Historic Site in the Big Horn

National Forest, are a few log foundations and miscellaneous scrap metal.

Which mining town lost the majority of its residents when saloons were closed?

Rudefeha, located on the Continental Divide near the town of Battle in southern Carbon County, was all but abandoned when residents banned saloons within the town limits. Owners of the mining company moved a mile west to establish Dillon, which soon became the largest Sierra Madre Mountains town. Foundations of log cabins still remain along the road that leads north out of Copperton Junction, or Forest Road 862.

Which Hot Spring County ghost town is filled with the remains of its children, attesting to harsh living conditions?

Gebo, Wyoming, in the northeastern section of Hot Springs County, contains a few standing walls of rock houses. Many of the former residences were dugouts with piles of rocks at the entrances. Only a few pieces of mining equipment remain as well as timbered mine shafts. The nearby ghost town of Crosby is located in Coal Draw south of Gebo. Both towns supplied coal to the town of Thermopolis during the 1890s. All that remains of Crosby is a house, mining structure, and tailings pile. Coal mines in the area closed in 1932.

Which mining town is considered one of Wyoming's best preserved ghost towns?

Mineral Hill in Crook County is located half a mile southwest of Welcome, a discontinued post office named for Welcome Gulch, an old mining camp. The former mill still stands and is sometimes operational, but the rest of the town is deserted. A number of buildings inhabit the area, including at least six mine buildings on Spotted Tail Creek and a number of old abandoned houses.

Which Teton County ghost town is now the site of a tourist cyclist route as well as a popular location for photographers?

Antelope Flats was settled in 1893 by Kansas pioneers who abandoned the area because the climate was too cold to grow crops. All that remains of the ghost town is a structure called Teton Barn, located thirteen miles from Jackson, Wyoming. Renowned western artist Conrad Schwiering built his home in the area and painted landscapes of the Teton Mountains from his yard.

Which town was established next to a sacred Shoshone burial ground site?

The town of Neiber housed a railroad station, post office, and general store, and was named for the area's first postmaster, Mary M. Neiber. Shoshone tribal members had previously held ceremonies nearby to honor their dead. Located in Washakie County nine miles south of Worland on US Highway 20, the former town site is situated off state Highway 431 West, just past the junction of Gooseberry Road.

Which Wyoming ghost town was once the center for relocated Japanese during World War II?

Heart Mountain was the relocation center for more than 10,000 Japanese residents from 1942-1945. The center contained churches, a fire station, hospital, and two movie theaters. Those housed at the center were allowed to work as field hands to earn money and were sometimes given passes to visit the towns of Cody and Powell. The camp was abandoned at the end of World War II.

Which ghost town was proclaimed "Best in the World," by nearby residents?

The residents of Upton, Wyoming, are proud of their local tourist attraction, located a mile north of town. Old Town Upton, now a ghost town, can be seen from County Road 16 near the towns of Moorcroft and Newcastle. A number of buildings, including Upton's first jail and the fire hall, are still standing in the former Weston County town.

Which Wyoming town ceased to exist when the county seized its bridge across

the North Platte River?

Residents of Bessemer Bend, a small town twelve miles upstream from Casper, planned to house not only the Natrona County seat but the state capitol as well. Bessemer voters tallied 677 ballots during the 1890 election, which was several times the town's population, so the county seat was awarded to Casper, whose votes totaled 304. Both towns were charged with ballot box stuffing, but Bessemer's offense was more grievous. The following year the town ceased to exist when county officials seized the bridge across the North Plate River that linked Bessemer Bend with Casper, for unpaid taxes. Most residents then moved, most of them to Casper.

Cities and Towns

Which Wyoming town was known for its street cars, elaborate theaters, and a jail from which prisoners escaped?

Sheridan's Railway Company was established in 1910, and provided transportation to the mining camps north of town as well as Fort Mackenzie. The town was platted in 1882, with theaters built from its inception, including the elegant Italinate-Gothic Cady Opera House, that featured traveling troupes that performed plays and vaudeville acts.

For whom was Rawlins Springs named?

Rawlins Springs, later shortened to Rawlins, was named for Brigadier General John A. Rawlins, who was appointed chief of staff of the army under President Ulysses S. Grant, but died six months later in 1869 at the age of

38. Rawlins accompanied General Granville M. Dodge to the area, which was established in 1868 by the Dakota Territorial legislature that included the present Carbon, Natrona, and Johnson counties. Rawlins had hoped the dry climate would cure his tuberculosis. Upon Rawlin's death, General Dodge named the army post Fort Rawlins, which is located in current Carbon County. The town of Rawlins Springs was incorporated in 1886, with a population of 574, which included 81 soldiers as well as a great many railroad employees.

Which town became the largest cattle shipping point in Wyoming on the Union Pacific Railroad line during the late 1870s and early 1880s?

Medicine Bow was the largest cattle shipping center in the state on the Union Pacific, shipping an average 2,000 head daily. After the decline in cattle growing, the town became a center for wool shipping during the early 1900s.

How did the town of Greybull get its name?

The town took its name from the Greybull River, which was reportedly named for an albino bison. Located at the confluence of the Greybull and Big Horn rivers in what is now Big Horn County, the region is rich in historical events. The county's Pryor Mountains were named for Nathaniel Pryor, a member of the Lewis and Clark

Expedition, and contains Bad Pass Trail, through which mountain men transported furs. The trail is said to have been used for 10,000 years by Native Americans and was mapped by John C. Fremont's expeditions, which took place from 1842-1854 with guides Kit Carson and Cimineau Lajeunesse, for whom the Seminoe Mountains were named.

For whom was the town of Jackson named?

Jackson's postmaster, Margaret Simpson, grandmother of former U.S. Senator Alan Simpson, named the town for David Jackson, an Ashley Fur Company partner. The town was platted in 1897 by Margaret and John Simpson as well as Robert and Grace Miller. Jackson became the Teton County seat when the area was formed from northern Lincoln County.

Where was Wyoming's first territorial prison located?

Wyoming Territorial Prison was established in Laramie City in 1872. The facility was approved by the territorial legislature in 1869, and was designed to house forty-two of the territory's felons. Deputy U.S. Marshal Nathaniel Boswell served as the first warden and the penitentiary charged the territorial government a dollar a day for each inmate, although the state of Nebraska only charged forty cents a day. The state of Illinois offered to house the inmates at no charge. As a result, most inmates were shipped to Joliet, Illinois, and the few who remained at the Wyoming territorial facility were allowed to visit Laramie on a Saturday night.

When was the railroad town of Casper established?

The railroad town was established in 1888. The first Fremont, Elkhorn, and Missouri train pulled into the station on June 15 of that year to a boisterous welcome. Railroad gypsies, who moved from one new town to the next, were unaware that Casper was the end of the line. The town was platted that fall and 25 by 100 feet business lots were sold for $200-$250 by the Carey Brothers and the railroad.

Which Wyoming town replaced Donkey Creek as the northeastern railhead?

Gillette was founded in 1891 when the Chicago, Burlington, and Quincy Railroad arrived in the area that is now Campbell County. A fairly lawless town, Gillette served as an entertainment center for railroad workers. Its train station was originally planned to be built at the tent city of Donkey Creek by railroad surveyor and engineer, Edward Gillette, who located a shorter route. Before long Gillette housed a commissary, seven saloons, and three dance halls catering to railroad construction crews. But as the railroad moved west, the town

Wyoming Historical Trivia

shrank to less than a third of its original size. It did remain, however, a railhead from which cattle and sheep were shipped to market.

Which gold mining town first produced railroad ties?

Centennial, a settlement established in 1868 to supply railroad ties to the Union Pacific, was homesteaded in 1869, but abandoned due to conflicts with the Indians. Seven years later, gold was discovered in the area and the Centennial Mine was named in honor of the nation's hundredth anniversary.

Which Wyoming town owes its existence to Fort McKinney on the Bozeman Trail?

The town of Buffalo sprang up three miles from Fort McKinney in what is now Johnson County. Surprisingly, the town's name was not derived from the plains bison but was chosen by a drawing. One of the town's residents reportedly wrote the name of his hometown of Buffalo, New York, on the slip of paper that was drawn.

Which town in the western section of the state was named for a railroad engineer?

Evanston, located in the southwestern corner of the state, was named for James A. Evans, a Union Pacific division engineer. The town was established in November 1868 to house Union

Pacific construction crews. It became a division point, which ensured the town's permanence. Lumbering was also established in the area to provide the railroad with ties. The production of charcoal was another industry developed in Uinta County for use in smelters near Salt Lake City.

Which town was first called Shoshone?

Cody, Wyoming, named for William F. "Buffalo Bill" Cody was originally called Shoshone. The name was rejected by the postal service, however, because it was too similar to the existing town of Shoshoni. Cody was platted in 1895, and the first building was constructed the following year.

Which western Wyoming town was known as "Never Sweat?"

Settled during the 1870s, the town of Dubois was first known as "Never Sweat," but when the town fathers applied for a post office, Washington officials decided the town should be named for Fred Dubois, a United States senator from Idaho and member of the Postal Committee. Among Dubois' early residents was Butch Cassidy, who operated a horse ranch in the area.

For whom was Kemmerer named?

Kemmerer was named for a Pennsylvania coal magnate named Mahlon S. Kemmerer, who bankrolled the Kemmerer Coal Company in 1897. Kemmerer also served as president of the Wyoming and Missouri Railroad, which transported coal from Wyoming's Black Hills.

Which Wyoming town advertises itself as the Jackalope capitol of the world?

Douglas adopted the Jackalope, a mythical jackrabbit with antlers, as its symbol. The animal can be found in numerous places within the city and along Interstate 25. Douglas is also the permanent site of the Wyoming State Fair and is in close proximity to Fort Fetterman, established eleven miles north of the town in 1867. Douglas was later founded in 1886.

A town was named for which Wyoming man who had acquired Native American artifacts from as far north as Alaska?

Frank S. Lusk established a ranch near the east-central Wyoming border in 1880. Six years later he helped to bring rail transportation to the area and donated a portion of his land for the town that would bear his name. Lusk traveled extensively and collected many Indian artifacts from not only the plains tribes but the southwest and Pacific Coast as far north as Alaska. He donated his collection to the State of Wyoming in 1921.

Which central Wyoming town evolved from an important Mormon emigrant

way station?

Glenrock, founded in 1886, was originally an important way station for emigrants traveling the Oregon-Mormon trails. Established in 1847 by the Latter Day Saints, it was the location of a 300-year-old buffalo jump site where Indians trapped and killed bison for food and clothing.

Which Wyoming town hosts an annual two-shot goose hunt?

Torrington hosts the annual two-shot goose hunt in December. Goshen County's Annual Sportsmen's Invitational attracts hunters, artists, and tourists nationwide, and has often been attended by Wyoming's governors and other well known people.

Residents of Tubb City abandoned their town to move to which eastern Wyoming railroad site?

Newcastle was founded in 1889 by J.H. Hemingway, superintendent of the Cambria Coal Company, who named the site for his hometown in the British Isles. Residents of Tubb City moved to the new town when it was learned that the railroad had decided to build its tracks through Newcastle instead.

Where is the annual one-shot antelope hunt held?

Lander's One-Shot Antelope Hunt, held during

September each year, draws celebrity sportsmen from around the nation in an attempt to bag a Wyoming antelope with a single shot. Governor Dave Freudenthal succeeded in 2004 as did U.S. Senator Mike Enzi with his father's World War I rifle.

Which railroad town decreased in size when it was learned that the railroad was establishing a division point further west.

Green River City was established in 1868 when the Union Pacific Railroad arrived. The area was still a part of Dakota Territory. Several men decided to operate businesses in the new town, including a mercantile, hotel, and restaurant, expecting the railroad to make the town its next division point. Some 2,000 railroad followers inhabited tents and adobe buildings in Green River City until it was announced that the proposed town of Bryan had been chosen as the railroad's terminus point. Most of the town's residents followed the tracks west toward Bryan and Bear River. The town of Bryan was later rejected due to a lack of water.

Which U. S. president's paternal grandfather owned and operated a mercantile store in Shoshoni, Wyoming?

Charles Henry King relocated his mercantile business from Douglas and Fetterman City to Shoshoni, a railroad town established in 1904.

His grandson, Leslie Lynch King, born July 14, 1913, was adopted at the age of two by his stepfather who changed his name to Gerald Rudolph Ford, Jr. Gerald Ford served as the thirty-eighth U.S. president from 1974-1977, following the resignation of Richard Nixon.

Which Wyoming town was originally a way station in what early teamsters considered a nightmarish desert region?

Rock Springs was originally a way station in 1862 after Ben Holladay's Overland Stage Line was moved to southern Wyoming to avoid constant Indian attacks in the northern part of the state. The town was established six years later when the Union Pacific Railroad laid its tracks through the area.

Wyoming Counties

How many counties exist in Wyoming?

The state's twenty-three counties are Albany, Big Horn, Campbell, Carbon, Converse, Crook, Fremont, Goshen, Hot Springs, Johnson, Laramie, Lincoln, Natrona, Niobrara, Park, Platte, Sheridan, Sublette, Sweetwater, Teton, Uinta, Washakie, and Weston.

Which counties are the largest and smallest?

Sweetwater County is the largest in the state with 10,425 square miles. Hot Springs County is the smallest with just over 2,003 square miles.

Which Wyoming county is home to the state's only university?

Albany County is the home of the University of Wyoming. The county was named by a member of the Dakota legislature for his former home in Albany, New York, before Wyoming became a state. The city of Laramie is the site of the university.

Which county was named for its Rocky Mountain sheep?

Big Horn County was named for the Bighorn or Rocky Mountain sheep, which were numerous in the area. The county was formed in 1896 with the town of Basin as its county seat.

For whom was Campbell County named?

Campbell County was named for two men: Robert Campbell, the partner of fur trader and mountain man, William Sublette, as well as John Campbell, Wyoming's First Territorial governor, who served from 1869 until 1875. Campbell County was created from the western sections of both Weston and Crook counties.

Which southern Wyoming county was home to the world's longest and highest aerial tramways?

The discovery of copper in southern Carbon County in 1897 led to the establishment of the Rudefelta, or Ferris-Haggarty mine, where the world's longest tramway was built using 370 towers that ranged from 10 to 70 feet above the ground and reached an elevation of 10,700 feet. The tramway was considered a wonder of the age when it was built at the turn of the twentieth century. Ore was transported from the Rudefelta mine in Battle, Wyoming, to the smelter in Riverside, a distance of sixteen miles. Carbon County was named for the extensive coal deposits in the area.

Which county was home to Deer Creek Station, built to accommodate Oregon Trail emigrants?

Deer Creek Station was built in what is now Converse County, and served as a mail and stage station as well as a supply station for emigrants traveling west. More than 350,000 travelers passed through the valley where Glenrock is now located. Converse County was named for A.R. Converse, a Cheyenne banker and stockman.

Where did the last Indian battle occur in Wyoming?

The Battle of Lightning Creek was fought in southern Weston County on October 20, 1903. Sheriff William Miller and his posse attempted to arrest Chief Charley Smith (Eagle Feather) and his band from the Pine Ridge Agency in South Dakota for game violations and the killing of range cattle. A dozen Sioux were arrested and the posse chased the larger band of twenty braves and thirty of their women, whom they overtook on Dry Fork of the Cheyenne River. A battle ensued, resulting in the deaths of Sheriff Miller and a posse member. Five Sioux were also killed. The rest escaped to the reservation after twenty-one were apprehended by Crook County Deputy Sheriff Lee Mather and a posse, but due to a lack of evidence, the game violators were freed. Crook County was named for General George Crook, a famous Indian fighter.

Which Fremont County town was chosen the county seat in 1884?

Lander was appointed the county seat when Fremont County was formed in 1884. The town was named for Frederick W. Lander. His 1859 expedition was responsible for construction of the Lander cutoff to Soda Springs, Idaho. Settlement didn't occur in the Lander area until 1869 when Camp Augur was built although oil had been discovered in the Wind River Basin by Captain Bonneville in 1833, and gold by John C. Fremont during his 1842 expedition. Fremont County was named for General John Charles Fremont.

Which county seat claims the world's largest mineral hot springs?

Thermopolis in Hot Springs County is known as home to the world's largest mineral hot springs. Shoshone and Arapaho tribes signed a treaty in 1896, allowing public use of the "healing waters." Ageless mineral deposits have created a rainbow-colored petrified "waterfall" which also draws tourists from across the nation to visit Hot Springs State Park.

Which county received its name from the bible as well as a French trapper?

Goshen County was organized in 1911 and contains the towns of Hawk Springs, Huntley, LaGrange, Lingle, Torrington, Veteran, Yoder, and Fort Laramie. The name Goshen originates from the biblical Land of Goshen. The county was also reportedly named for a French trapper whose name was Gosche.

Which county ranks first in population in the state?

Laramie County, located in the southeast corner of Wyoming, shares its eastern border with Nebraska and southern border with Colorado. Cheyenne, the state capitol, ranks first in population in the state as does Laramie County, although it only ranks fifteenth in size among Wyoming's twenty-three counties. Laramie was named for Jacques LaRamie, a French-Canadian trapper who was killed by warriors near the army post that was later named for him, Fort Laramie.

Which Wyoming county was named for a Cheyenne lawyer?

Johnson County was the site of many famous Indian battles, the Johnson County Cattle War, and the Bozeman Trail. The area was inhabited by homesteaders, outlaws, ranchers, and miners. Named for a Cheyenne lawyer, E.P. Johnson, the county is home to the small towns of Buffalo and Kaycee. Buffalo is the county seat.

Which county was named in honor of our sixteenth president?

Lincoln County was named for Abraham Lincoln, who served as the sixteenth U.S. President. Organized in 1911 with Kemmerer as the county seat, the following towns took root within its borders: Afton, Alpine, Diamondville, Northeast Auburn, Bedford, Cokeville, Grover, Etan, Fairview, Fontenelle, Kemmerer, Smoot, LaBarge, Oakley, Opal, Star Valley, Taylor, Thayne, and Turnerville.

Which Wyoming county was named for its extensive soda deposits?

Natrona County was named for its trona, or soda deposits. Carbon was roughly split in half to form Natrona County in 1890, allotting Natrona 5,500 square miles with Casper as its county seat. The area was the site of an emigrant resting area on the Oregon and Mormon trails as well as Fort Caspar. The army post was established on the Platte River to guard the transcontinental telegraph line and Overland Mail Service.

Which county was claimed by five nations and was once a part of three counties?

Wyoming Historical Trivia

Park County was once included in Sweetwater, Fremont, and Big Horn counties until the state legislature set aside the boundaries of Park County in 1909, naming the area for Yellowstone National Park. Before Wyoming became a territory, the land was once variously claimed as territories of Spain, Great Britain, Mexico, France, and the United States. It was then for a number of years a part of Dakota Territory. The town of Cody was named the county seat and the courthouse was completed in 1912.

Which Platte County town was an early cattle growing center?

Chugwater, settled in 1867, became an early center for stock growing, including the huge Swan Land and Cattle Company of the 1880s. The town apparently was named for nearby Chugwater Creek. Legend has it that "chug" meant chimney or chimney rock, which is located north of town. Platte County received its name from the river, which originates from the French word plate, meaning dull or shallow.

Which county is the site of the Bradford Brinton Memorial Historic Ranch that houses artwork of Charles M. Russell and Frederic Remington, among others?

Sheridan County, named in honor of Civil War General Phillip Sheridan, is the site of the Bradford Brinton Museum, which recreates ranch life of the Old West. The western art collection includes sculptures, paintings, and etchings by such artists as Charles M. Russell, Frederic Remington, Edward Borein, and Frank Tenney Johnson. There is also a large collection of plains Indian crafts, rare books, and documents, as well as the twenty-room main house and reception gallery.

In which Wyoming county is the town of Purple Sage?

Purple Sage is a town of less than 500 residents, with an average resident age of 25. The town is located in Sweetwater County between Rock Springs and Green River. Organized in 1867, the county was named for the Sweetwater River. More than a hundred miles of the Oregon, California, Mormon, and Pony Express trails still remain relatively untouched within the county, and parallel Highway 28. Sweetwater County is known as the world's trona capital. Processed into soda ash, the mineral is an ingredient in toothpaste, glass, and baking soda. The county is also known for its Red Desert and Flaming Gorge recreation area. Green River is the county seat.

Which Wyoming county borders both Utah and Colorado?

Uinta County in the southwestern corner of the state, is one of Wyoming's smallest counties and was established in 1869. Its towns include

Evanston, Carter, Fort Bridger, Lonetree, Lyman, Mountain View and Robertson. The county was named for both the Uintah Mountains and the Uintah Indian tribe. Evanston, located along Interstate 80, is the largest town and the county seat. Fort Bridger and Bear River State Park are also located there.

Which Wyoming County contains only three towns within its boundaries?

Washakie County, named for Shoshone Chief Washakie, is home to Ten Sleep, Winchester, and Worland. The county was created in 1911 from part of Big Horn County, with Worland as the county seat. Early towns included No Wood, Colter, Nieber, Red Bank, and Rome. When he was born around the turn of the nineteenth century, Chief Washakie was named Pina Quaah. The noted warrior who became the Shoshone chief was an ally of the white man and sought to acquire better living conditions for his people, including hospitals, schools, and churches. The chief also granted the Union Pacific Railroad the right-of-way through Shoshone land in western Wyoming.

Which county borders both Montana and South Dakota?

Crook County, in the Wyoming's northeastern corner, borders both Montana and South Dakota. The county was organized in 1875 with Sundance as the county seat. Crook County is located in the Black Hills. Its county seat lies at the foot of Sundance Mountain, where Sioux Indians still hold their religious ceremonies and councils at Wi Wacipi Phaha, otherwise known as the Temple of the Sioux.

Who bought ranch land in 1926 that became Grand Teton National Park?

John D. Rockefeller bought land from Buffalo Fork to the Gros Ventre River. Congress then designated the land as the Jackson Hole National Monument in 1929. Ranchers battled politicians over grazing and hunting rights, which were later restored. Congress abolished the monument in 1950 and incorporated Grand Teton National Park, along with additional Rockefeller land purchases. Teton County, of which the park comprises more than a third of its land, was named for the Teton Mountains, which the area natives called Tee-win-ot or Three Pinnacles. French trappers called the mountains Les Trois Tetons. The county was organized in 1921.

Which county, located on the west side of the Rocky Mountains' Continental Divide, is 80% public land?

Sublette County, home to about 6,000 residents, is made up of BLM, state, and Bridger-Teton National Forest land. Located seventy miles south of Jackson, the county contains the headwaters of the Green River. Wildlife includes mule deer, antelope, elk, moose, grizzly, black bear, and wolves. The area was first inhabited by Crow, Shoshone, Gros Ventre, Sheepeaters, and Bannock tribes. Trappers and explorers arrived during the early 1800s and were later replaced by cattlemen and ranchers. Pinedale was platted in 1899 and became the county seat in 1926.

Who discovered coal in Lincoln County, which led to the establishment of the town of Glencoe?

The William Ashley and Andrew Henry expedition of 1822 discovered coal in the area, but it was not until 1894 that mining operations began. A miner named the settlement Glencoe after a town in his native Scotland. A number of mine accidents killed over a hundred miners before the town of Glencoe was abandoned during the early 1940s, when the coal supply became scarce.

A former state legislator threatened a shootout over which new county?

Niobrara County was formed in 1911 from eastern Converse County, although there was much opposition to the split. The editor of the Manville Register was opposed to the new county, and former state legislator Nat Baker reportedly threatened a shootout if Niobrara County became a reality. The name Niobrara originated with the Niobrara River, which in the Omaha Indian language means flat or broad river. Niobrara County is located in the eastern central region of Wyoming, and borders both Nebraska and South Dakota. Lusk, the county seat, is in the southern part of the county.

Wyoming Water

Which Wyoming reservoir was named for John C. Fremont?

Pathfinder Dam in Natrona County was named for John C. Fremont, who was known as "the great pathfinder." He explored the Wyoming wilderness, extensively mapping the region. Construction of the reservoir began in 1905 and was completed in 1909 with a holding capacity of one million acre-feet of water, of which the state of Nebraska received the lion's share.

Which Wyoming town celebrated its new piped-in water supply by crowding the local saloons?

Casper volunteer firemen first shot a stream of water 120 feet into the air, ripping shingles from roofs. They then joined other residents by drinking the town dry. They stood six deep before the bar in succession at all nine saloons. Within three years, alkali had eaten holes in the water pipes, which sprung hundreds of leaks between Elkhorn Creek and Casper. They were replaced with cast iron pipes in 1902-1903.

Which reservoir was named for the state's most well known developer?

Located west of Cody in the upper Shoshone Valley, the Buffalo Bill Dam was first called the Shoshone Project. The initial construction was approved and funded in 1904, and the dam was at that time the largest federal project in Wyoming and the highest reservoir in the world in 1910 when it was completed. The reclamation project encompasses 93,000 acres, providing irrigation water for such crops as hay and sugar beets. Originally conceived by William F. Cody and his partner, it was turned over to the federal government when the entrepreneurs ran out of money.

Which river was said to be an inch deep and a mile wide?

An old Wyoming adage was "Powder River, an inch deep, a mile wide. Can't swim it nor can't wade it." The western edge of the Powder River is bordered by the Big Horn Mountains and flows south from the Cloud Peak Wilderness area. Considered sacred ground by Native Americans, the Powder rises in the foothills of Wyoming's Big Horn Mountains and flows north 486 miles to the Yellowstone River near Terry, Montana. Crazy Woman Creek and the Little Powder River are tributaries.

Which Wyoming river's French name means "beautiful fork?"

Belle Fourche (pronounced Bell Foosh) is a French name that means "beautiful fork." The Belle Fourche River originates in the Wyoming plains and slowly makes its way into South Dakota through historic country. The river is located near Devil's Tower, where fishing has been reported quite good during the cooler seasons. The Belle Fourche River is the lowest elevation in the state at 3,100 feet.

Where is Wyoming's largest lake?

Yellowstone, Wyoming's largest lake, lies in the northwest corner of the state. The lake covers 131 square miles and has a depth of up to 300 feet. A fault area in the northern part of the lake is roughly 2,000 feet long and rises 100 feet above the lake bottom. The area includes craters and many hot springs southwest of Storm Point.

Where is the state's second largest lake?

Fremont Lake, the second largest in Wyoming, is located near Pinedale. Twelve miles long and half a mile wide, the lake has been known to give up forty-pound fish. Summer and winter fishing derbies are held each year as well as a sailing regatta.

Which river flows through the gap between the Owl Creek Mountains and the Big Horns?

The Bighorn River is a tributary of the Yellowstone and is 460 miles in length. The water's upper reaches are called the Wind River and becomes the Bighorn when it approaches the Owl Creek Mountains. The river runs through the gap between the Big Horn and Owl Creek Mountains and is referred to by some as the Wind-Bighorn. One of its forks becomes the Little Wind River near Riverton, Wyoming, and Boysen Reservoir is the source of the Bighorn River in the Owl Creek Mountains.

Three states fought long and hard over which river water?

Preparations for the Alcova irrigation project were taking shape in 1920, and the *Casper Daily Tribune* was reporting that 100,000 to 125,000 acres of land would be reclaimed along the North Platte River above and below the city of Casper. The area was to be devoted to the cultivation of 50,000 acres of alfalfa, 11,000 acres of sugar beets, 15,000 acres of small grains, and the rest in potatoes, corn, pasture, and truck gardens. But the $23 million Kendrick Project would not become a reality until 1941 because the states of Nebraska and

Wyoming Historical Trivia

Colorado opposed the water project. Wyoming senator John B. Kendrick lobbied long in Washington for the reclamation project, but his efforts were stymied by Nebraska's demand for enough irrigation water for 800,000 acres of farmland. Colorado wanted its Transmountain Diversion Project, and Wyoming lobbied for 150 million kilowatts of power to supply the state with electricity as well as its planned agricultural projects. But there simply was not enough water in the North Platte River to serve all the states. Wyoming eventually received the smallest allotment of water.

Which rivers did John Wesley Powell and his men navigate in 1869 in small wooden boats?

John Wesley Powell sailed downstream during spring of 1869 with nine other men in small wooden boats to explore the Colorado and Green rivers. When Powell saw the sun reflecting from the orange-red rocks, he named the area Flaming Gorge.

Which state reservoir holds the record for the biggest walleye caught?

A Boysen Reservoir angler holds the record Walleye catch of 17 pounds, 6 3/4 ounces. The 19,000 acre reservoir provides good fishing and water recreation, including ice fishing during the winter months. Located about a hundred miles west of Casper and twenty miles from

Thermopolis, the dam is situated near the southern end of Wind River Canyon and can be accessed by both highways 20 and 26 on its southern and eastern boundaries.

Which two rivers join in northwestern Wyoming to form a major confluence and white water rafting areas?

The Hoback and Snake Rivers converge in northwestern Wyoming to form one of the state's major confluences and white water rafting areas. Hoback Canyon, through which the river flows, also offers rock climbing. The canyon is sometimes blocked by winter avalanches but is a unique place to view wildlife, including moose, deer, and bighorn sheep. Snowmobiling and dog sled teams to Granite Hot Springs are available during the winter months. A side trip from Granite Creek provides breathtaking views of the Gros Ventre Range and the 50-foot Granite Waterfall.

Wyoming Mountains

In which order did the Rocky Mountain ranges form in Wyoming?

The Rocky Mountains formed slowly at the end of the Mesozoic period. The first ranges to form were the Granite, Wind River, and Medicine Bow followed by the Tetons and Gros Ventre ranges. Then rose the Owl Creek, Beartooth, western Gros Ventre, Washakie, and Big Horn ranges as well as the Black Hills.

Which mountain range emerged as the state's most recent, following millions of years of volcanic eruptions?

Only the tallest peaks of mountains buried under thousands of feet of ash and lava were visible after millions of years of volcanic eruptions. By the end of the Cenozoic period, new volcanic eruptions occurred along the northwest side of the Tetons and a fifty-mile crack appeared. A fault then rose on the range's western side as the eastern side dropped. The Tetons were thus formed.

In which mountain range is Togwotee Pass located?

Togwotee Pass is located in the Wind River Mountains of western Wyoming, which range for more than a hundred miles from north to south. Wind River Mountains represent one of the largest wilderness areas in the nation and is relatively devoid of roads. More than 1,600 lakes in the region contain various species of trout. Still abundant in the area are big game animals including elk, mountain lions, moose, deer, bighorn sheep, grizzlies, bobcats, and wolves.

Which national monument stands on the northwestern-most point of Wyoming's Black Hills?

Theodore Roosevelt designated Devil's Tower the first national monument in 1906. Located at the northwestern tip of Wyoming's Black Hills, the rock formation is considered a sacred place by American Indians. Tourists visit the site and rock climbers scale the vertical walls. The Black Hills are actually mountains situated in the northeastern corner of Wyoming, which extend into northwestern South Dakota. Their western elevations rise to 7,000 feet. Forty miles of maintained trails connect to 295 miles in South Dakota. The Wyoming trails can be accessed through Sundance and Newcastle.

Which mountain range encompasses the Medicine Bow National Forest?

The Laramie Mountains, an eastern section of the Rockies, range east and west in southeastern Wyoming from Casper Mountain in the north to northern Colorado and eastern Albany County, Wyoming. Laramie Peak is the highest point at 10,272 feet and the range of mountains encompasses, in part, Medicine Bow National Forest.

In which mountain range is the Cloud Peak Wilderness area?

The Big Horn National Forest of north central Wyoming encompasses Cloud Peak Wilderness area. Located halfway between Yellowstone Park and Mount Rushmore, the area includes canyons, waterfalls, grasslands, reservoirs, lakes, forest and desert land, glacial valleys, and sheer rock walls, as well as 1,500 miles of trails in the 189,000 acre wilderness area. Although no paved roads cut through the Cloud Peak Wilderness area, it can be accessed to the north from Dayton and Shell, and from the south from Buffalo and Ten Sleep.

Which mountain range is located on the east of Yellowstone National Park?

The Absaroka Range spans 150 miles on the eastern edge of the Rocky Mountains, forming the boundary for Yellowstone Park. Sub-ranges include the Beartooth Mountains with peaks higher than 12,000 feet.

Which mountain range was named for one of Wyoming's mountain men?

The Bridger Mountains, named for trapper Jim Bridger, is a short sub-range of the Rockies. The mountain range is a bridge between the Bighorn Mountains to the east and the Owl Creek Mountains to the west. The Bridger Mountains reach an elevation of 8,359 feet.

Which ranger district is divided in two by the Wind River Reservation?

Named for Shoshone Indian Chief Washakie, the ranger district is located in western Wyoming, and divided into two areas by the reservation. The Continental Divide separates the Bridger-Teton National Forest from the Washakie Ranger District. The Washakie Wilderness Area was established in 1972 in memory of Chief Washakie, and was taken from the South Absaroka Wilderness and Stratified Primitive Area. The Wilderness area has deep, narrow valleys that feature the southern Absaroka Mountains' volcanic strata. The volcanic material is deposited in horizontal layers and is unstable and erodible, creating irregular buttes and cliffs such as the Pinnacles at Brooks Lake near

Dubois. Petroglyphs and artifacts are evidence that Fremont Indians hunted game near the mountain range shared with northeastern Utah. Later, the Ute, Comanche, and Shoshone tribes ranged throughout the mountain region of Flaming Gorge. The Uinta Mountains are the only major east-west mountain range in North America.

Which northwestern Wyoming ski area has temperatures ranging from -30 to 30+ degrees during December through May?

Beartooth Mountain elevations in the northwestern section of Wyoming range between 7,500 and 11,000 feet and experience a 60+ degree temperature range. The ski area, with thirty-two miles of groomed trails and thirty-four miles of additional trails, has three to ten feet of packed powder. The season runs from December through April, but riding continues through May. Facilities, services, and rentals are available in Cody and Powell, Wyoming, as well as Cooke City, Montana. The Beartooth Highway, which passes through Custer and Shoshone National Forests, is sixty-five miles in length and closes from mid-October until May.

Which mountain range is within the Wind River Reservation in its entirety?

The Owl Creek Mountains in central Wyoming

are part of the Rocky Mountain range and are situated entirely within the reservation. The range is bordered on the east by the Bridger Mountains, the northwest by the Absaroka Range, and the north by the Bighorn Basin, which form the boundary between Hot Springs and Fremont counties. Within the range is Copper Mountain which has scattered deposits of copper, gold, silver, tungsten, beryl, iron, spodumene, and uranium. The major copper producer, the DePass mine, developed some 11,000 feet of tunnels and shafts and shipped an estimated 567,610 pounds of copper during 1906, 1917 and 1918, along with gold and silver.

Which mountain range is home to three ranches in Natrona County?

The Rattlesnake Mountains are owned or leased by the Dumbell and Circle Bar ranches, and Clear Creek Cattle Company in the region southwest of Casper. The Dumbell Ranch was established during the 1880s and operated as a cattle ranch with both private and public leased land. The Circle Bar Ranch was homesteaded by Emma Clayton in 1894 and has been in the family for over a hundred years. Most of the deeded land was acquired by consolidating homesteads, and BLM land was acquired over a period of time. Clear Creek Cattle Company is a family-owned corporation founded in 1906 by William Hendry, a Scottish immigrant. The JE Ranch, located south of Highway 20/26, was purchased by the Clear Creek Cattle Company in 1981, and was part of the Matador Cattle Company. A public and private access for hunting has been available upon request for several years.

In which mountain range have rubies, jasper, sapphires, and a 200-pound jade stone been found?

A ruby deposit with a strike length of 5,000 feet was discovered in the Granite Mountains of central Wyoming, and a jade specimen as heavy as 200 pounds has been unearthed as well as other precious stones. Located north of Jeffrey City and east of Lander, the Granite Mountains are 3.6 billion years old.

Which mountain range has a French name that means "big belly"?

Gros Ventre is a French word that means "big belly," and originates from sign language that meant Indians were constantly hungry. The Gros Ventre Mountains of Sublette County became a part of the National Wilderness Preservation System in 1984, and the 300,000 acres are part of the Bridger-Teton National Forest. The higher elevations are usually snow-free by the middle of July and accessible until mid-September. The elevation ranges from 7,000 feet to over 11,000 feet, and afternoon thundershowers are not uncommon during the summer months. Snow can fall at the higher elevations at any time of year.

J. J. Hammond

In which Wyoming mountains was the Grand Encampment District established in 1902?

The Grand Encampment Mining District was established following the construction of the aerial tramway in 1902 in the Sierra Madre Mountains in the southern part of the state. Reaching an elevation of over 10,000 feet at its highest point, the tramway ran sixteen miles from the Ferris-Haggarty Mine to the copper smelter at Riverside. Built at a cost of over $350,000, the tramway contained 370 towers and sixteen tension stations to maintain some 300,000 feet of steel cables. The first of 985 ore buckets arrived at the smelter during January 1903. Copper ore had previously been hauled in freight wagons following the discovery by a sheepherder in 1897. Mining towns were soon established as hundreds of miners arrived in what became known as the Grand Encampment.

Wyoming Historic Sites

When was the first governor's mansion built in Cheyenne?

Constructed in 1904 and listed on the National Register of Historic Places since 1969, the original governors' mansion has hosted a number of visiting dignitaries, including U.S. presidents and vice presidents. The red brick colonial mansion was constructed for $40,000 (including the cost of land), and was officially dedicated during January 1905. The governor's mansion opened to the public as an historic residential museum in 1977.

Which army fort was built along the Bozeman Trail on former Lakota and Cheyenne buffalo hunting grounds?

Fort Phil Kearny, located near Story, Wyoming, replaced Fort Reno near Kaycee in 1866, sixty miles to the south. Built on the Lakota Sioux and Cheyenne Indians' buffalo hunting grounds, the fort's purpose was to prevent intertribal warfare and to draw attention away from construction of the intercontinental railroad across southern Wyoming. The Fetterman Battle and Wagon Box Fight took place within the fort's brief existence. Fort Phil Kearny, along with Fort Reno and Fort C.F. Smith in Hardin, Montana, were abandoned in 1868 following the Fort Laramie Treaty, which banned army posts north of the Platte River.

Which historic monument was partially destroyed by Fourth of July celebrants in 1847?

Portions of Independence Rock were blown away with gunpowder by exuberant emigrants from a thousand-member wagon train in 1847. Other celebrations included weddings at the rock that reaches 193 feet at its highest point, 1,950 feet in length, and 850 feet in width. Thousands of names were chiseled and plaques embedded by the Latter Day Saints as well as Natrona County's service organizations, which commemorates the monolith's importance as a resting place along the Oregon, California, and Mormon trails.

Which historic site houses the state's territorial prison?

Wyoming Territorial Park in Laramie is the site

of Wyoming's restored territorial prison. Listed on the National Register, the prison was built in 1872, and held some of the most notorious outlaws in the region, including Butch Cassidy. The 190-acre facility features the Ranchland Exhibit, Frontier Town, Horse Barn Dinner Theater, and the Happy Jack Gift Shop.

Which historic site was the scene of the Battle of Tongue River?

The Connor Battlefield historic site is located near Ranchester and Interstate 90 north of Sheridan, Wyoming. The Battle of Tongue River took place between General Patrick Connor's troops and Black Bear's Arapaho tribe during August of 1865. Camping, fishing, and picnicking areas are available along the Tongue River.

Which historic site, considered one of the most authentic in the nation, was once a boom town?

South Pass City boomed in 1867 when gold was discovered in the southern Wind River Mountains. More than a thousand miners and their families took up residence by the following year. South Pass City hosts an annual Gold Rush Days the last Friday, Saturday, and Sunday in July to celebrate Sweetwater Mining District heritage with a number of activities, including a vintage baseball tournament with period equipment, uniforms and rules. A hand-drilling competition is also on the agenda when men attempt to out-drill one another with a two-ton granite block in single and double jacking events. The South Pass City staff and Wyoming State Parks and Cultural Resources conduct an ongoing joint effort to restore the remaining original buildings.

Which historic army post was located within Wyoming's "Wind Corridor?"

The Fort Fred Steele historic site is within the southern Wyoming wind corridor along Interstate 80, which encompasses the area from Rock Springs to the region north of Laramie. The fort once guarded the Union Pacific Railroad from possible Indian attacks for twenty years until 1886. Wildlife is still plentiful in the area, including deer and antelope.

Where can you find nineteenth century footprints as well as wagon ruts?

Oregon Trail Ruts historic site is located a mile south of Highway 26 near the town of Guernsey, Wyoming. Ruts in the area are two to six feet deep and footprints are clearly visible beside the wagon ruts in an eroded sandstone ridge on the south side of the North Platte River. The Oregon Trail ruts are evidence of the route followed by hundreds of thousands of travelers in their western migration between 1841 and 1869. Trails in the area are self-guided with no available facilities.

Where is the Register Cliff site?

Much like Independence Rock, Register Cliff is one of the best preserved sandstone boulders where emigrants carved their names, dates, and messages to let friends and family following on the Oregon Trail know when they had reached that point in the trail, or simply to let others know they had been there. The historic site is adjacent to an emigrant campground about a day's trek west of Fort Laramie. The graves of three unknown emigrants are located below the cliff and surrounded by an iron fence.

Which historic fort catered to a wide variety of travelers on the Oregon Trail?

Fort Bridger was established as a small fort by Jim Bridger and his partner Louis Vasquez, with a blacksmith shop and supplies for emigrants traveling past the Black Fork of Green River. The small fort existed a mere decade, but while it lasted, it served as one of the main stopovers on the Oregon-Mormon trails and catered to mountain men-trappers, Indians, and explorers, as well as Mormon travelers from the time it was built in 1843. The fort also catered to the army, railroad, and pony express riders. A number of events are now held at the fort, including The Mountain Man Winter Encampment at the Bridger's Post replica, the annual Mountain Man Rendezvous, Halloween tours of the fort, moonlight tours, and the annual Easter egg hunt.

J. J. Hammond

Which historic site is the former home of governor and U.S. Senator John B. Kendrick?

The Trails End Historic Center of Sheridan features an early twentieth century lifestyle and contains many of the Kendrick family's furnishings and personal effects. An orphaned Texas cowboy, John B. Kendrick arrived in the state with a cattle drive and became both a Wyoming governor and U.S. senator. He is also credited with the establishment of the Alcova Reservoir Project in central Wyoming, and for his fight to retain Wyoming's rightful share of water during the 1930s.

Where did 10,000 years of habitation come to light under 26 feet of earth and rocks?

Medicine Lodge, located on the western slope of the Big Horn Mountains, is known for its native American petroglyphs and pictographs as well as 10,000 years of continuous human habitation. The site wasn't fully unearthed until 1969, when Dr. George Frison, Wyoming state archeologist, began a series of digs in the Big Horn Basin.

National Parks, Forests, and Monuments

Which national park was the first to be designated in the United States?

Yellowstone was the first national park established in this country, and is among the largest with 2,221,733 acres of land that overlaps into Montana and Idaho. David Thompson, an explorer and geographer for the Northwest British fur trade is credited with naming the Yellowstone River in 1797, in notes he made while visiting Mandan villages on the upper Missouri. John Colter, the first white man to encounter present Yellowstone Park in 1807-1808, was not believed when he later described the area. Jim Bridger visited the Yellowstone area in 1830 and his descriptions were also not believed because his reputation was that of a storyteller. It wasn't until the 1860s and 1870s when several expeditions to Yellowstone mapped the region, that Colter and Bridger's descriptions of the geothermal wonders were taken seriously. President Grant designated the area as a national park in 1872.

Which mountain range encompasses an active fault block and eight peaks over 12,000 feet?

Grand Teton National Park, located in northwestern Wyoming, is a 40-mile long mountain range with an active fault block. The park is home to elk, mule deer, antelope, black bear, and buffalo, as well as grizzlies in the northern regions. The mountains rise out of the sagebrush flats without foothills to block the magnificent view. Eight mountain peaks reach over 12,000 feet, Grand Teton the highest at 13,700 feet. The backpacking trail runs north from the park's southern boundary to Paintbrush Canyon for thirty-nine miles and is a three-day hike through the high country where more than 300 species of birds can be seen.

Which national forest is sandwiched between the towns of Sheridan and Greybull?

The Bighorn National Forest encompasses 1.1 million acres of Big Horn Mountains in north-central Wyoming. The towns of Lovell, Greybull, and Worland are located to the west, while Sheridan and Buffalo lie to the east of the national forest, which also borders Montana.

The diverse landscape was valued by the Crow, Sioux, Eastern Cheyenne, and Arapaho, and for its varied species of wildlife. A number of battles were fought with the United States military in the foothills and surrounding areas of the Big Horn Mountains.

Which national forest does Wyoming share with the state of Utah?

Wyoming shares Ashley National Forest with northeastern Utah. The 1.3 million acre reserve encompasses the northern and southern slopes of the Uinta Mountains, Tavaputs Plateau, and the Wyoming Basin. The main section of Flaming Gorge Reservoir extends ninety-one miles with over 300 miles of shoreline, lodging, marinas, rapids, and boat ramps. Fishing and water sports are abundant in the recreational areas, but the 460,000-acre Ashley National Forest lies mainly in northeastern Utah.

Where are the Vedauwoo rocks and the Devil's Playground located?

Medicine Bow National Forest in south-central Wyoming includes the majority of the Medicine Bow and Laramie Mountains as well as the Snowy Range. Formations unique to the area include the Devil's Playground (a pile of granite boulders) and the Vedauwoo rocks. The Snowy Range Scenic Byway winds through the forest where camping and picnic sites are available along with many other attractions. Hikers may access the highest point in the park, Medicine Bow Peak, which is 12,013 feet in elevation. The byway is open from late May though the month of October. Savage Run, Hustun Park, Platte River, and the Encampment River Wilderness areas provide opportunities for horseback riding, snowmobiling, motorcycling, and cross country skiing as well as fishing and hunting.

Where is the largest National Forest in the contiguous forty-eight United States?

Bridger-Teton is the largest national forest with 3.4 million acres, and is second only in area to Alaska's Tongrass and Chugach national forests with an area of 22.6 billion acres. Included in the forest are the Teton, Gros Ventre, Wind River, Salt River, and Wyoming Mountain ranges. The national forest is the largest area of undeveloped land in the contiguous U.S. Many hiking trails are available as well as mountain climbing to the state's highest point, Gannet Peak at 13,804 feet. There's also an abundance of navigable rivers and lakes within the forests, which provide opportunities for recreational boating, rafting and sport fishing. Wildlife abounds in the region, including grizzly bear and over 350 species of birds.

Which National Monument is sacred to Native Americans?

The 1,267 foot monolith near the Belle Fourche River is located in the northeastern Wyoming

Black Hills area and is the considered a remnant of a volcanic eruption. Devil's Tower National Monument was the first to be so designated by President Teddy Roosevelt in 1906, and encompasses 1,347 acres of park land, which includes forests, grasslands as well as abundant wildlife. The tower was known to a number of northern plains tribes as Bear's Lodge and is considered a sacred site of worship. The tower was also the setting for the film, "Close Encounters of the Third Kind." A campground with fifty sites is available in the park, as well as opportunities to hike, view wildlife, picnic, and take pictures.

Which national monument features the richest fossil deposits in the world?

Located in southwestern Wyoming fifteen miles west of Kemmerer on Highway 30, Fossil Butte National Monument dates back fifty million years and is one of the world's richest fossil beds. More than seventy-five fossil displays include the oldest known bat specimen and 356 species of fish as well as a 13-foot crocodile. The Fossil Lake Trail is a mile and a half in length and winds among aspens and samples of wildlife and local geology. The two-mile Historic Quarry Trail features wayside exhibits of high desert plants and wildlife. A moderately steep side trail leads to an historic quarry and a variety of birds and wildlife may be viewed in the area. A picnic area is available.

J. J. Hammond

Which national forest encompasses five wilderness areas and three mountain ranges?

Bordered on the west by Yellowstone National Park, the Shoshone National Forest stretches from the Montana border to Lander, Wyoming, including sections of the Absaroka, Wind River, and Beartooth Mountain ranges. The national forest was designated in 1891 with 2.4 million acres of land ranging in elevation from 4,600 to 13,804 feet, including the state's highest point, Gannett Peak. Abundant backpacking trails exist along with deer, elk, black bear, bighorn sheep, and grizzlies. Rafting is available at Clark's Fork Canyon as well as hiking, camping, biking, and picnicking from Memorial Day to September 30. Snowmobiling and skiing are also available from early December through late April on more than 300 trails.

Wyoming State Parks

Which state park was named for a man who spent twenty years as a guide for Wyoming hunting parties?

Buffalo Bill State Park was named for Colonel William F. Cody, who served not only as a hunting guide, but a pony express rider, showman, developer, and promoter. He established the town named in his honor and helped to bring agriculture and irrigation projects to the area. A portion of the land now occupied by the Buffalo Bill State Park was once owned by Cody and sold to the government for the reservoir project, which began in 1905.

Which state park was originally land reserved by treaty for Sioux tribes until the gold rush of 1874?

Keyhole State Park was Sioux land by treaty

with the U.S. government until the Black Hills gold rush of 1874. Confrontations with miners and emigrants resulted in the loss of Sioux land in the area. The state park was later designated and named for the Keyhole livestock brand used by the McKean brothers who ranched nearby. Located in the northeastern corner of Wyoming, the park contains a reservoir and nearly 15,000 acres of water recreation.

Which state park features a river that sinks into cave fissures?

Sinks Canyon State Park was named for the Middle Fork of the Popo Agie River, which flows through the canyon from the Wind River Mountains. Halfway down Loops Road is Sinks Canyon where the river disappears into a large limestone cavern and reappears half a mile downstream. The state park offers hiking trails, fishing, wildlife viewing, and bird watching as well as the river's unusual sinks and rises.

Which state park is located within a Wyoming city's limits?

Located within the Evanston city limits, Bear River State Park features abundant wildlife, which includes a herd of bison and elk. Hiking, skiing trails, picnicking shelters, and a slow moving river are all available at the park. Established in 1991, Bear River State Park is situated within Uinta County in southwestern

Wyoming. Native Americans, who previously lived in the area, named the river Quee-ya-paw for the tobacco that grew along its banks. Fur trappers renamed it Bear River because of the large bear population in the area. No camping is allowed in the park.

Which Wyoming state park was named for a native born sportscaster?

Designated near Cheyenne in 1971, Curt Gowdy State Park, was named for the famous broadcaster who grew up in Green River, Wyoming. The area was originally a favorite camping ground for a number of Indian tribes, including the Shoshone, Comanche, Pawnee, Sioux, Arapaho and Crow, who hunted bison throughout the region. Curt Gowdy Park was established through a lease agreement with the Boy Scouts and the City of Cheyenne, and is maintained by the Wyoming Department of State Parks & Cultural Resources. Recreational activities include camping, fishing, boating, wind surfing, and wildlife viewing.

Which state park is the result of work by the Civilian Conservation Corps?

Guernsey State Park was created by the Civilian Conservation Corps (CCC) workers in 1933. Bridges, roads, and hiking trials were built as well as a museum, castle, Brimmer Point, and a nine-hole golf course. The dam was completed in 1927 by the Bureau of Reclamation, which created Lake Guernsey, an excellent site for fishing, swimming, and boating. The museum offers a number of displays and other buildings include the castle with a giant fireplace and winding steps to an observation area. Picnic shelters are also available.

Which state park maintains its bath house at a temperature of 104 degrees?

The Hot Springs State Park in Thermopolis maintains its hot mineral water at 104 degrees and limits soaking time to half an hour for safety reasons. Some of the most beautiful flower gardens in the state are planted in the park, and the famous swinging bridge has undergone recent repairs. The Hot Springs State Park buffalo herd roams free within the park boundaries for most of the year, with the exception of summer months when they are confined to a corral. Three picnic shelters are available by reservation and a newly built boat ramp is located on the Bighorn River by the terraces.

Which state park lies between the northern and southern Oregon Trails along the North Platte River?

The 315-acre parcel, named for a twenty-five-year Wyoming legislator, was transformed from a former rock quarry to a park with roads, walking trails, areas for fishing, boating, and canoeing. Edness Kimball Wilkins State Park, located in Natrona County, six miles east of Casper, lies between the Oregon Trail's Council Bluffs Road to the north and the main trail, which runs south of the park off Highway 20-26. The Oregon Trail runs parallel to the highway but wagon ruts are not visible from the road. Fishing, picnicking, walking trails, and bird watching are among the activities available at the park.

Which state park was named for the French trapper-scout, Basil Cimineau Lajeunesse?

The Seminoe State Park was named for the Seminoe Mountains, which were in turn named for Basil Cimineau Lajeunesse. The trapper and his brother discovered the tar springs, located in the Lander area, and sold the petroleum as axel grease for wagons and as a lubricant to protect the feet of oxen and cattle traveling the Oregon Trail. The Lajeunesse brothers later served as scouts for the U.S. Army and were present at Platte Bridge Station in the current Casper area in 1865 when Red Cloud's warriors attacked and killed a number of soldiers. The Lajeunesse brothers, whose mother was Cheyenne, were sent out from the fort that night to notify officials at Deer Creek to send reinforcements to Platte Bridge Station, which was later renamed Fort Caspar in honor of the young slain lieutenant. The Americanized spelling of Basil Lajeunesse's French name is Seminoe, hence the park's name. Seminoe State Park is the site of good fishing and boating as well as wildlife viewing. The area, surrounded by the Seminoe Mountains, was also once a gold prospecting site during the late 1800s.

Which state park contains a series of dunes that reach as far as the sand hills of Nebraska?

The Glendo State Park is located in one of Wyoming's historic regions. The Spanish Diggings lie a few miles east of the reservoir and suggest early habitation. Also on the reservoir's east side is a series of sand dunes that stretch from the Green River and Great Divide Basin to the Nebraska sand hills. Indian artifacts from the Sioux, Arapaho, and Cheyenne tribes have been found in the area as well as wagon tracks from the Oregon, Mormon, and California trails although most of them are now under water. The fertile earth attracted farmers and ranchers to the area and some of the best potatoes were once grown in the Glendo area.

Early Communications and Newspapers

Which form of communication initially linked the civilized regions of wilderness Wyoming?

The Pony Express was established April 3, 1860, to provide mail delivery service between Sacramento, California, and St. Joseph, Missouri. The route traversed Wyoming, where a series of relay stations were built. One hundred eighty-three relay riders rode day and night, seven days a week, for a period of just over 18 months between the eastern and western terminuses of the transcontinental telegraph line offices, which were under construction to provide communication between the East and West coasts. The trips usually took ten days in summer and twelve to sixteen days during winter, if riders or their horses were not killed by Indians or inclement weather. When the transcontinental telegraph line was completed during October 1861, the Pony Express service was terminated, but the stage had been set for the transcontinental railroad by 1869.

Which newspaper is Wyoming's oldest?

The *Wyoming State Tribune* published its first newspaper in 1867 before Wyoming became a territory, and has not missed an issue since. The Republican oriented newspaper was first called *The Cheyenne Leader* and was a daily. It was consolidated by the Cheyenne Newspapers Group with *The Wyoming Eagle* and is now known as *The Wyoming Tribune-Eagle*.

Which publisher named his newspaper in honor of his pet mule?

Bill Nye named the Republican newspaper he established in 1881 *The Laramie Boomerang* for his pet mule, but the humorist first served as postmaster of the southern Wyoming town. His work has been compared with that of Mark Twain and much of the journalist-author's work sold quite well during the early days of Wyoming's territorial existence. The *Frontier Index* was Laramie's first newspaper, published briefly in Laramie in 1868 by a former telegrapher traveling with the Union Pacific Railroad, which moved west as tracks were laid. *The Laramie Daily Sentinel* then set up business from 1869-1895 and was followed by *the Laramie Independent* in 1871, and later renamed the Daily Sun. A political paper, *The Laramie Daily Chronicle*, was also published briefly in 1871.

Which newspaper was older than the city in which it was located?

The Rock Springs Miner, founded in 1881, is older than the city itself. *The Miner* later merged with *The Rock Springs Rocket*, which was originally called *The Independent* and founded during the early 1880s. The mining camp of Rock Spring (later changed to Rock Springs) was set up in 1868 by Charles Wardell and William Mellor for the Union Pacific Railroad. Both the newspapers, prior to their merger, reported on the Chinese Massacre of 1885.

Which homesteader wrote to *the Casper Daily Mail* to complain about the "land grabbers" who attempted to block the formation of Natrona County?

James Averell, who was hanged with his wife Ellen as a result of his letters to the editor, wrote a lengthy complaint February 7, 1889 to the editor of *the Casper Daily Mail*. Cattlemen then kidnapped and hanged the Averells the following July in Sweetwater Valley. To excuse their crimes, they spread rumors that Averell's wife had received stolen cattle in exchange for her favors. Thus, she became erroneously known as "Cattle Kate." Brand papers and a bill of sale were later found for the cattle after the couple's deaths in Ellen "Ella" Watson-Averell's safety deposit box in Rawlins. Witnesses to the murders disappeared and the cattlemen were exonerated. A.J. Bothwell, who led the lynching party, then bought the Averell's homesteaded land, which adjoined his own grazing land, but not before there was condemnation in the newspapers across the nation for "the barbaric lynching of a woman in Wyoming."

Which small mining town newspaper often featured strange tales of the "Coogly Woo" and "One-Eyed Screaming Enu" in the editor's column?

Grant Jones published the first edition of *The Dillion Doublejack* in 1902 and regularly included strange tales of the "Coogy Woo," "Bockaboar," and "One-Eyed Screaming Emu" in his "Grant Jones' Anvil" column. His work was reprinted in newspapers across the country and Grant Jones was credited with attracting numerous miners to the area during the copper boom. But he unfortunately had a drinking problem and was found dead the following year after a 53-mile ride through a snowstorm.

Who drove through Wyoming's worst "blizzard of 1949" to buy the Riverton newspaper?"

Bob and Roy Peck drove from Laramie to Riverton during the worst snowstorm of the century to purchase a newspaper, *The Riverton Press*. Margaret Peck also accompanied her husband Roy during Christmas vacation of 1949, while Bob was in his senior year at the University of Wyoming. Both men previously worked for *The Riverton Review* and planned for a decade to publish a newspaper of their own. Renaming the newspaper *The Riverton Times*, the two men struggled with dilapidated equipment and merged four years later with *the Riverton Ranger*, which was a twice weekly newspaper.

Where was the *Weekly Grit* published?

The Worland Weekly Grit was first published in 1906 by Tom Daggett, who wanted to expand the newspaper into a daily serving the entire Big Horn Basin. It was not until 1939 that the Republican-oriented newspaper, the *Northern Wyoming Daily News* became a reality, 29 years after Daggett's death. Tracey McCracken and his partner Ted O'Melia, who owned several other Wyoming newspapers, purchased *the Grit* in 1938.

Which publisher lacked the money for stamps to bill his advertisers?

Tracy McCracken, who would later own a number of Wyoming newspapers, took over *the Wyoming Eagle* when it was a weak competitor of the

Cheyenne Tribune in 1926. McCracken worked as a one-man staff for 18 hours a day and found himself so broke at the end of his first month that he couldn't afford stamps to send bills to his advertisers. He delivered them all in person. By the end of the following year, he and the newspaper were out of debt and by 1933, McCracken was a power to be reckoned with in the state Democratic party. He cast Wyoming's deciding votes at the 1960 Democratic convention, which nominated John F. Kennedy for the presidency.

Which newspaper was established by a justice of the peace?

Judge Alden, Gillette's first justice of the peace, was reportedly the town's first newspaper publisher-editor in 1881, but no surviving issues have been found. S.D. Perry published the first issue of *The Gillette News* in 1904 and sold the newspaper to Roy Montgomery eight years later. Montgomery, a Democrat, ran his newspaper unopposed until 1913 when a Gillette businessmen's group financed *The Campbell County Record,* which expressed Republican views. Yellow journalism was rampant in both newspapers, and C.D. Perry, *The Record's* publisher, left to establish *The Republican* in 1921. Arthur Nisselius, a homesteader, bought *The Gillette News* in 1925 and combined it with *the Record.* He sold *The Gillette News-Record* within two years to McCracken Newspapers. Nisselius established another weekly in 1935, *The Campbell County Review,* but the following year, he again bought *The Gillette News-Record* and closed *down the Review.*

Which Wyoming newspaper auctioned off its first copy for $10 in 1898?

The Grand Encampment Herald was produced in 1898 by Drury Brothers Publishers. The first copy, which proclaimed the mining area of Encampment "the World's Store House of Gold, Copper and Cobalt," was auctioned off for $10 to Hank Ashley and is on display at the Grand Encampment Museum. The newspaper business was purchased for $50,000 by a French syndicate following the sale of the copper and cobalt mines.

Which *New York Daily Sun* news editor bought the weekly *Basin Republican-Rustler* newspaper?

Tom Daggett had previously worked as the assistant editor of the *New York Sun* before he traveled to the Big Horn Basin on assignment. There he met W.A. Richards who published *The Rustler.* Daggett purchased *The Rustler* from Richards and moved the newspaper to Otto, Wyoming, where he renamed his newspaper *The Big Horn County Rustler. The Basin Republican* was established in 1928 after *The Rustler* began leaning to the left. In a speech to the Basin City Rotary Club, Ed Phillips, a later publisher, told members that early newspapers were all political and if someone wanted to run for office, he could start one of his own, usually for as little as $1,000.

Which weekly newspaper changed towns as well as names after taking delivery of Buffalo Bill's print shop equipment?

Major Burke took delivery of the printing equipment freighted in from Sundance in 1888 because Bill Cody wasn't around to pay for it. He then started his own *Shoshone Valley News*, which he moved to another town where the paper became *the Meeteetse News*. The News merged with the *Cody Ent*erprise in 1932.

Which newspaper operated without electricity and further from any railroad in the nation?

C. Watt Brandon was lured to Pinedale, then called Pine Creek, in 1904 by his cousin Charles Patterson, whose family was platting the new town. C. W. Brandon managed to enlist 283 subscribers for his proposed newspaper at $2 a year, as well as a number of advertisers in Rock Springs, Green River City, Opal, Evanston, and Kemmerer. He then hitched up a sheepwagon to a team of horses and drove to Rock Springs to buy an old army printing press and supplies for $350, which he freighted the hundred miles home, a journey of six days. During his trip, he encountered quicksand and the Little Colorado Desert. The newspaper's first home was a log cabin with dirt floor where Brandon produced a handset four-page broadsheet without benefit of electricity. One of his lead stories concerned the Cumberland payroll robbery in Kemmerer, which was committed by three bandits, one of whom he later learned was a close friend.

Which newspaper office was set ablaze by an arsonist, resulting in two deaths?

An arsonist set *the Cody Enterprise* on fire in 1974, killing a young reporter in the basement photo lab and a fireman who tried to rescue him. Most of the equipment was destroyed. Newspapers in Lander, Riverton, Jackson, and Powell, Wyoming, offered help, as well as Billings and Red Lodge, Montana. *The Cody Enterprise* was originally founded in 1899 by William F. "Buffalo Bill" Cody and run during World War II by Milward and Lorna Simpson.

Who established the Powell Tribune?

S.A. Nelson, a school teacher, started the newspaper in 1909 when there were few businesses in Powell. Nelson was at the time publisher of *the Cody Enterprise* and commuted weekly to Powell by train to sell ads and learn the latest news. *The Powell Tribune* was printed in Cody until Nelson bought printing equipment in 1911 to publish the newspaper locally. In 1912, the newspaper sold to J. Rolla Baird, who became partners with A. S. Morse in 1915. Morse bought out his partner in 1916, but sold the paper to the Baird family less than two years later. Curtis and Dorothy Whaley bought the newspaper in 1955 from their in-laws and sold it to Roy and Bob Peck of Riverton in 1964.

Which newspaper carried the story of a "race for a bride" rodeo competition?

The Sheridan Enterprise in 1909 reported on its rodeo race, which offered a bride to the winning cowboy. Harry Lewis was the winner who swept Miss Hazel Foster of Rock Creek from the saddle and married her on the spot. *The Sheridan Enterprise* was established by Tom Tynan and Fay Sommers in 1887. A rival newspaper, *The Sheridan Post*, was founded in 1887 by Thomas Cotton, a young lawyer and former schoolteacher. *The Po*st merged with *the Sheridan E*nterprise in 1923 and was published as the *Sheridan Post-Enterprise. The Sheridan Journal*, a Republican paper, was started in 1923 by C. Watt Brandon to rival *The Democratic Post Enterprise which* sold in 1930 and became *the Sheridan Press,* which merged with its competitor, *the Journal.*

Where did *The Frontier In*dex, which traveled with the Union Pacific Railroad, derail?

Legh Freeman established *The Frontier Index*, a newspaper that traveled westward with the railroad as the transcontinental line was built across Wyoming in 1868. Freeman, a former telegrapher, published his newspapers at new railroad towns or camps until he reached Bear

Town, south of Evanston, where his printing equipment was destroyed by vandals.

Which eastern Wyoming newspaper had ads for $3 iron beds and $8 davenports on its front page in 1908?

The Torrington Telegram, established in 1907, published its advertising on the front page. Published every Thursday with E.E. Haring as its editor, the subscription rate was $1.50 a year. The four-page newspaper featured a prominent article on each page titled "Sparks from the Wire" that included messages from the subscribers to their friends. Prominent advertisements appeared on the front page for the first years of the newspaper's existence, along with the news in 1923 that a sugar factory was to be built in the area. The Holly Sugar Company continued as a major employer in Goshen County.

Which Uinta County publisher deserted his business after only a few months in 1871?

The Evanston Age, founded by W.L. Vaughn in 1871, was deserted after a few months when Vaughn packed his clothes and left town. Two years later, William Wheeler took possession of the printing press and resumed publication. By 1875, *The Evanston Age* was a daily paper with an annual subscription rate of $10, but by the following year, the newspaper was published three times a week for a $5 annual rate. That same year, Wheeler formed a partnership with William Shafter, who owned the *Green River Rocky Mountain Courier* and *the Rawlins Carbon County Ne*ws. Consolidating the three newspapers, the two men worked as partners until Wheeler moved to Idaho two years later after closing down *The Evanston Age.*

Which frontier paper began in Tubb Town, a temporary railroad settlement?

The Field City Journal, also known as *The Stockade Journal,* was first published in Tubb Town and printed on an army cylinder press in a board shack in 1889. When the railroad bypassed Tubb Town, residents deserted to Newcastle where the first lots were being sold. There the newspaper relocated and became *the Newcastle Journal.* The following year, Judge F. H. Fall started the Newcastle News which merged in 1892 with *The Journal.* In 1924, *The News Journal* merged with *The Upton News Letter* and *The Tribune* to form *The News Letter and News Journal.* A rival newspaper, *The Weston County Gazette* was founded in Newcastle in 1911, which moved to Upton in 1914. Three newspapers began during the early 1920s, when the oilfield boom took place in the Osage area. None survived after 1925.

In what area were *The Sundance Times* and *Moorcroft Monitor* simultaneously

published?

The Sundance Times and *The Monitor*, two politically opposed papers, were at constant odds before 1920. *The Times* originated in Moorcroft in 1913, but Joe Lytle moved the newspaper to Sundance late that year where he found the business activity more inviting.

Which Jackson newspaper's first issue sold out in a matter of hours.

The Jackson Hole Guide, published by Floy Tonkin, sold its first thousand copies in a matter of hours in 1952. *The Guide* was preceded by the Jackson Hole Courier in 1909 and *the Grand Teton newspaper*. Tonkin, a widow and veteran news woman, previously published the *Lingle Review* with her husband for 30 years. *The Guide's* heading until 1985 featured a pen and ink drawing of "Beaver Dick" Leigh by Albert Nelson, a local artist-rancher.

Which Platte County town published *The Uplift* during the 1890s?

Hartville, first Wyoming town to incorporate in what was then Laramie County, was the location of *The Uplift* newspaper. *The Uplift* moved to Guernsey around 1902 after the railroad arrived. The name was then changed to *the Iron Gazette* and eventually to the *Guernsey Gazette*. George Houser moved his family from Illinois to Guernsey after he bought the Gazette in 1913, and was a strong proponent of the formation of an Iron County to be formed from northern Laramie County. When the county was established, however, the name was Platte.

Which northern Wyoming weekly paper claimed to be "Republican in politics, progressive in principle?"

The Buffalo Bulletin's first issue in 1884 boldly stated its politics as well as the fact that it was the first newspaper published north of the Platte River. The Johnson County newspaper was founded by Joe DeBarthe and Charles Lingle. and DeBarthe served as editor. The *Bulletin's* predecessor, the *Big Horn Sentinel*, was founded in Big Horn in 1884 and moved to Buffalo three years later. In 1892, the Bulletin reported on the events of the Johnson County War. Other early publications included bitter competitors, *The Buffalo Echo* and *The Buffalo Voice*. *The Voice* was silenced during the 1920s when it was purchased by *the Bulletin*.

Which weekly publication billed itself as "Wyoming's Picture Newspaper"?

The *Wyoming State Journal* in Lander billed itself as "Wyoming's Picture Newspaper" and was one of the first in the world to convert to desktop publishing. The multi-award winning newspaper traces its roots back to 1887 when Isaac Wynn founded *The Fremont Clipper* after serving as the editor of *The Wind River*

Mountaineer. The Clipper's masthead included the publisher's son, although Ed Wynn left the Lander area for a while to work for other newspapers. The elder Wynn reportedly never missed a chance to ridicule in print his former employer, W. B. McKenzie, the owner of *The Mountaineer,* who lived in the Denver area, but Wynn eventually settled down to respectable news reporting. *The Clipper,* with Republican leanings, became the official Fremont County newspaper. Over the years, the Lander newspapers included *The Fremont Clipper, The Wind River Mountaineer,* and *Wyoming State Journal.*

Which weekly publisher claimed to have run all of his competitors out of town?

He called his newspaper *Bill Barlow's Budget* until his death in 1919, and was said to have run all his competitors out of Douglas, Wyoming. He was also known for drinking his friends under the table. Bill Barlow was a pen name. The publisher's real name was Merris C. Barrow and he hailed from Nebraska. His sole office staffer was his wife Elizabeth, whom everyone called Mrs. Bill. When Barrow established his newspaper in 1884, he was convinced that Douglas would become "the great Wyoming metropolis" and Barrow went after competing newspapers with a vengeance. *The Douglas Republican, Central Wyoming News, Converse*

County Press, Rowdy West, and *the Douglas Advertiser* ceased publication and left town by the year 1898. *The Budget* went through a series of owners and was purchased in 1985 by Sage Publishing Group.

How many Glenrock newspapers have been published in Converse County since 1886?

The Glen Rock Graphic published news of the area from 1886 until 1892. *The Vortex* started up the following year and lasted until 1895. There were no further newspapers until *the Glenrock Review*, which was published from 1911 until 1913. *The Glenrock Derrick* only lasted a few months during World War I, although *the Glenrock Gazette* was more fortunate for it was in operation from 1916 until 1924, when it merged with *the Green River News. The Glenrock Independent* began business in 1922, but a fire during the mid-1930s destroyed early copies of the newspaper as well as its records. Nerwin O. Reed took over as publisher in 1939, and remained on the job until just before his death in 1996 at the age of 96. Reed's newspaper policies once cost him his gasoline credit card due to his stand on the mineral severance tax issue.

Which weekly paper did P.P. Anderson and F.F. Bristow purchase?

The Wyoming Standard newspaper of Greybull

was founded in 1907, the same year as the town, by R.S. Woodward. Typesetting was done by hand and the press was also hand operated. The newspaper sold within three months, which began a series of owners and a name change to *the Greybull Standard* in 1916. During 1919 the weekly sold to P.P. Anderson and F.F. Bristow. In 1923, *the Greybull Standard* merged with *the Greybull Tribune*, and the name was changed to *the Greybull Standard and Tribune*. The newspaper was one of the first in Wyoming to convert to web offset printing in 1966, and was sold to Sage Publishing in 1978.

Which newspaper was billed as "The big farm and home newspaper of Goshen County"?

The Lingle Guide, founded in 1917 by C.R. Spencer as *the Lingle Review*, experienced a number of name changes. During the 1920s it was *The Family News Review* but soon switched back to *The Lingle Review* when the second owners, Leo Tonkin and his wife Floy purchased the newspaper in 1926. When her husband died in 1933, Mrs. Tonkin published the newspaper with her son Jack, who served as editor. *The Guide-Review* sold in 1948 to the Keith Rider and Edwin Lebsock of Torrington, who switched formats from broadsheet to tabloid, and reduced the issues from twice to once a week.

What conservation-oriented newspaper set up shop in a town of 2,300 where there was already a newspaper?

The Jackson Hole News was founded in 1970 by two diversely opinionated publishers. Ralph Gill, a conservative, and Virginia Huidekoper, a liberal, published their new weekly on Thursday, the same day as *the Jackson Hole Guide,* and shared their opposing viewpoints with the community. Within the first year, Gill sold his interest to one of their reporters, Marc Fischer, who then became co-publisher. His partner, Virginia Huidekoper, a photographer as well as a perfectionist, insisted on quality although the newspaper's equipment was badly outdated. During the summer, the tabloid ran twenty-four pages, which shrank to sixteen during the winter. The newspaper sold to its young reporter, Michael Sellet, in 1973. Under his direction, *the Jackson Hole News* won hundreds of awards and was named the nation's top weekly newspaper by the National Newspaper Association.

Which weekly retained its original name from 1906?

The Lovell Chronicle may be the oldest newspaper in the state to have retained its original name. Printing equipment was hauled into town in 1906 from Montana by wagon, and the inexperienced publisher, J.P. May, sold out to W.M. Jones two years later. Jones left town shortly thereafter, however, when the Lovell Commercial Club persuaded him to turn over his newspaper to them. Editor and printer, Reyn Leedom was then imported from Kansas to run *the Chronicle*. Under his direction, the town gained a professional publication and the newspaper purchased new equipment. One of Leedom's special editions featured construction of a sugar factory in 1917 and promotions of a glass factory, brick and tile plant, as well as civic improvements. Roy and Bob Peck purchased the newspaper in 1970 and added it to their news group.

Which newspaper was known nationally for its colorful and political reporting?

The Lusk Herald published its first issue in 1886 in the tent town of Silver Cliff, Wyoming. Its publisher was J.K. Calkins. The town was then named for F.S. Lusk, one of its most respected citizens. *The Herald* sold within a year to the typesetter, James Mayes, who owned the publication until 1914. *The Herald* was later owned by J.B. Griffith, Sr., who married former publisher, Martin Agnew's widow in 1926 and bought out the remaining partner. Griffith, Republican state chairman in 1940, and later state commissioner of public lands, took over management of *The Lusk Herald* in 1941, and was nationally known for his colorful journalism and political views. In 1957, his son Jim took over the newspaper.

Which two newspapers gave birth to *The Kemmerer Gazette* in 1924?

The Kemmerer Camera had its start in 1901 when Patrick J. Quealy bought printing equipment from *The Diamondville News* and hired the editor, George McArthur, to publish his paper. Seven years later, an experienced newsman, C. Watt Brandon, arrived from Pinedale to publish *The Camera*. Then *The Kemmerer Republican* came into being in 1912 with Lester G. Baker as its publisher. The rival newspapers merged in 1924, when the two weeklies became one daily as *The Kemmerer Gazette*, under the direction of Lester C. Baker, who served as the Republican state and county chairman as well as a state legislator, and mayor of Kemmerer during the 1920s.

What newspaper was originally planned to be published in Hanna, Wyoming?

*The Medicine Bow Po*st, established by David Roberts in 1977, was originally planned for Hanna, but when he stopped at the Virginian Hotel in Medicine Bow and discussed the town's assets, Roberts decided to stay. A recent journalism graduate, he found that financing was difficult but was able to secure a loan with a bank in Nebraska. When he began publishing *the Post*, preliminary work was being done on the Medicine Bow Wind Energy Project, which was phased out by the Reagan administration. Operating on a slim budget with ancient equipment, Roberts managed two years later to found *the Hanna Herald* with editor, Velene Cormier. The young publisher also helped to organize the Medicine Bow Chamber of Commerce and establish the local museum. As editor-publisher, his weekly won numerous state and national press awards for excellence. In 1988, Roberts offered his newspaper to the University of Wyoming, which accepted on behalf of its journalism department.

Who was called "The Grand Old Man of Wyoming" by the Press Association?

J.A. Stewart, who purchased *The Moorcroft Democrat* with Fred Guthery in 1921, was referred to as "The Grand Old Man of Wyoming" because of his dedication to the newspaper business as well as the welfare of his readers. His wife continued as publisher in 1929 upon Stewart's death, and his son served as manager of the weekly *Moorcroft Leader* (renamed in 1924). The town's first newspaper, *The Moorcroft Times*, was founded in 1909 by Charles Shelling, and soon had competition in 1910 by *The Moorcroft Blade*, owned by E.J. McKinney. *The Times* became *The Democrat* in 1914 with Charles McKee as publisher.

Which newspaper reported from the state's southeast corner?

The Pine Bluffs Post newspaper, in Laramie County's southeastern corner, was considered a questionable venture in 1908, but R D. Wilson of the *Kimball Observer* in Nebraska decided a newspaper was needed across the southern Wyoming border. He hired veteran editor, Fred Mathias, to establish *the Post*. The area was newly settled by homesteaders that year in the area called "the Golden Prairie." Many articles were first published about farming techniques of homesteaders and of the publisher's struggle to keep his newspaper afloat. *The Post* sold in 1914 to the Hemphills, a father and son team and to George Reed two years later. Reed then sold the newspaper to J.R. Parish, a Newcastle subscriber, in 1928.

Which editor called himself "The Sage Brush Poet?"

Frank Burdick was the second editor of the *Weston County Gazette,* founded in 1915. Burdick assumed command of the newspaper in 1921, and was the self-proclaimed "Sage Brush Poet," who included samples of his work in selected editions of the Upton, Wyoming, weekly. Democratic in its early years, the Gazette switched parties in 1934 and acquired the first typesetting plant in northeast Wyoming following a devastating fire in 1931.

Which Platte County paper routinely employed the old "stock trick?"

The Wheatland Times, like other small town newspapers, would print one copy of its current edition with a front page story designed to embarrass one of its citizens, usually someone who did not want his name in print. The "victim" was unaware that his copy was the only one in existence, however. Exaggeration and humor made the articles interesting, according to a former *Times publisher*. The newspaper published its first issue in 1901 as the *Laramie County Times* prior to Platte County's formation. Less than three years later, the publisher, George Carroll, moved to Cheyenne to work for the railroad and later as a Laramie County deputy. The newspaper's name was changed in 1913 to *The Wheatland Times* just prior to Laramie County's split into three separate counties. Joe Johnson, publisher, touted his weekly as having the largest circulation of any county paper in Wyoming.

Which newspaper did "the lurid liar of Lander" publish? And who were the first women to later publish the newspaper?

Col. J.F. Crawford, editor and proprietor of the *Platte Valley Lyre*, later renamed *the Saratoga Sun*, was known to fellow residents as "the lurid liar of Lander," a nickname from which he took no small amount of pride. He began publishing in 1888 but soon sold to W.B. Hugus, who in turn sold to Gertrude and Laura Huntington in 1890. The Huntington sisters were the first women in Wyoming to own and operate a newspaper and became known as the "Lyre Girls." Laura

Huntington Heath served as business manager and Gertrude as the Lyre's editor. They set type by hand and reported on events such as the Ferris-Haggerty mine discovery, which put nearby Encampment on the national map. In 1891, George Canis started *the Saratoga Daily Sun*, but changed it to a weekly after the first issue. Canis sold *the Sun* the following year to J.F. Crawford, founder of *the Lyre*, and the two rival newspapers battled it out in print until 1902, when the Huntington sisters sold their newspaper to W.B. Wiley, who changed the Lyre's name to *the Saratoga State Record*. Crawford bought *the Record* later that year and merged it with his *Saratoga Sun*.

Which early publisher merged three newspapers that he started in the same town?

Fred Winchester published his Republican newspaper, *The Thermopolis Record*, in 1901, but sold the weekly and created a bi-weekly, which he named *The Thermopolis Independent*, which sold two years later. He then left journalism for twenty years. In 1930, Winchester acquired yet another newspaper, *The Thermopolis Reminder*, which became *The Journal*. *The Journal* was sold within two years to Ralph Noble, son of the former *Independent* owner. Winchester ran *The Journal* with J.E. Monger. *The Journal* competed with another publication, *the Thermopolis Daily Record*, which appeared in 1931. The only newspaper to survive, *The Thermopolis Independent Record*, is a conglomerate of the previous papers, with the exception of the town's first weekly, the short-lived *Big Horn River Pilot*, which was founded in 1895.

Which western Wyoming newspaper lost its early issues to both fire and floods?

The Star Valley Pioneer lost all its early editions from 1901 through 1915 to fire or flood, so reconstructing its history is difficult. *The Pioneer* was founded in 1901 by Emil Vaterlaus and his brother Conrad, with Conrad serving as publisher-editor. The name was changed to *The Star Valley Independent* in 1904 and sold to Henry Billings a couple of years later. Typesetting was done by hand until 1915, when a linotype machine was placed in operation by the publisher, Clyde Settle. Located in an eastside basement, *The Independent's* linotype machine had to be operated late at night or early mornings because the power surge would otherwise overtax Afton's limited power supply. Since that time, *The Independent* has won a number of first awards for excellence as well as the Hanway Plaque for outstanding Wyoming weekly newspapers.

Wyoming Disasters

Which Mormon emigrants failed to survive because they left Iowa too late in the year to avoid Wyoming's severe fall weather?

During the fall of 1856, two groups of Mormon handcart companies traveling to Salt Lake City from Iowa, were caught in an October blizzard after they crossed the North Platte River at Fort Caspar. Traveling separately and numbering about 500, were members of the Howard Martin and James Willie companies. They were low on provisions and warm clothing. Within nine days, fifty-six people with the Willie company perished in the vicinity of present day South Pass City. The Martin company lost many of its members in the vicinity of Devil's Gate and Independence Rock before help arrived from Salt Lake City.

Where did the largest landslide in the nation occur?

The Gros Ventre landslide occurred in 1925 near the small town of Kelly in the vicinity of Grand Teton National Park. Heavy rains and melting snow caused land slippage, which sent an estimated 50,000,000 cubic yards of earth, trees, and rocks crashing across the Gros Ventre River. An earthen dam nearly 1,000 feet long and 225 feet high was created in the short span of a few minutes. The resultant lake, called Lower Slide, was 200 feet deep and three miles in length. Two years later, heavy spring runoff caused the earthen dam to break, drowning several people and destroying ranch buildings as well as the small town of Kelly.

Why did the 1885 Chinese Massacre happen in the Rock Springs area?

Frustrated by drastic pay cuts, Swedish and Welsh coal miners went on strike in the Rock Springs area and were replaced by Chinese workers. The unemployed miners rioted, killing or wounding 28 Chinese miners. They also burned the homes of many others before federal troops arrived to maintain order. The troops remained in Rock Springs until 1898.

Where have earthquakes occurred in the state?

Earthquakes recorded since 1871 have occurred

Wyoming Historical Trivia

in every county in the state. Tremors of 7.5 magnitude on the Richter scale are possible in the western section of Wyoming and 6.75 along the Wind River Basin, according to a U.S. Geological Survey report, which also states that earthquakes of 6.25 to 6.5 magnitude are possible elsewhere in the state. More Wyoming earthquakes have been recorded in Yellowstone Park than in any other area of Wyoming.

Which infamous Wyoming landmark was partially destroyed by a tornado?

Teapot Rock, located in northeastern Natrona County, lost its spout when a tornado dislodged some of its rocks. A temporary oil boomtown named for the monument was abandoned in 1925 following a disastrous fire and serious typhoid epidemic. Residents of Teapot moved a few miles north to a new location on the edge of Salt Creek Oilfield.

Which blizzard is the one by which all Wyoming snowstorms are judged?

The blizzard of 1949 is still the gauge by which all bad winters are compared. The storm isolated residents and travelers alike, many of whom did not survive the below-zero temperatures and blinding snow. Stock growers' losses totaled more than $10 million when 23,000 head of cattle and 125,000 sheep were lost, while wild game found their way into towns searching for food. Forty-mile-an-hour winds created ground blizzards and six feet snowdrifts piled up along roads and highways for two months.

Which boomtown suffered a disastrous fire and serious typhoid fever epidemic before residents moved away?

Those who survived both the epidemic and fire in the oilfield town of Old LaVoye in 1923 grudgingly gave up squatters rights to land leased by the Ohio Oil Company and moved a few miles north to a new location on the southern edge of the Salt Creek Oilfield. A similar disaster occurred in the nearby town of Salt Creek when the town's third major fire destroyed a block of permanent buildings, resulting in the town's demise. Lack of water and too few firefighters were blamed for the disaster.

Why did a $750,000 grasshopper bill pass the Wyoming legislature in 1950?

Governor Crane called for a special session of the legislature to appropriate funding to fight a bumper crop of grasshoppers, which ate nearly everything in their paths. Casper Air Base served as the control center for the new Wyoming Grasshopper Control Board, which spent more than $1 million to fight the insects statewide. Sixty trucks and forty planes were used to distribute 12,000 tons of lethal bait to combat the problem.

When did a devastating drought strike

Wyoming?

Wyoming suffered a devastating drought during the 1930s when crop prices plummeted, mines closed, and banks failed as the state suffered through the Great Depression. The state was fortunate, however, in that Wyoming's economy received a boost from increased oil production and various federal projects such as the Alcova, Kortes, and Seminoe Dams, as well as the Kendrick and North Platte River projects, which provided for hydroelectric power and irrigation water.

Which southern Wyoming coal mine claimed more lives in one explosion than any other?

Hundreds of miners were killed in southern Wyoming coal mines from the 1880s through the 1930s, but the Union Pacific mine in Hanna lost more than 170 miners in a single explosion in 1903.

Where is the longest migration route in the lower 48 states for endangered wild life?

The Upper Green River Valley is the longest big game migration route in the continental United States. It lies between Yellowstone and Grand Teton National Parks to the north and the Red Desert to the south, and is a crucial link that binds the Greater Yellowstone Ecosystem together.

The Green River valley is home to thousands of wildlife species, including the largest herd of mule deer in the nation, herds of pronghorn antelope, elk, golden eagles, peregrine falcons, burrowing owls, and sage grouse. With more than 100,000 big-game animals dependent on the valley for their survival, the area offers world-class wildlife viewing and hunting opportunities. The river valley is also the largest publicly owned big game winter reserve in the region, but the area also contains one of the largest natural gas reserves.

Modes of Transportation

Which mode of transportation created the need to form Wyoming Territory?

Construction of the transcontinental railroad was the primary reason Wyoming became a territory in 1869. Government officials feared that the Pacific Coast could not be defended against foreign occupation, primarily the British, unless a railroad line was constructed to carry troops and munitions to California and the Northwest. On May 10, 1869, the Union Pacific tracks were joined with the Central Pacific Railroad at Promontory, Utah, and the long-awaited coast-to-coast rail line was completed.

How did most people travel before the railroads were built?

Stagecoaches transported passengers before the transcontinental railroad linked the East with the West. The heavy Concord Stagecoach was first manufactured in New Hampshire, in 1827. The stagecoach's ability to survive rugged terrain was due mainly to its thoroughbraces, or multiple leather straps, on which the coach rocked. The Wells Fargo stagecoaches were also built in New Hampshire by J. Stephens Abbott and his wheelwright, Lewis Downing, who perfected their high, wide design to handle the rough, rutted roads. The curved body frame provided strength, and allowed passengers room. The formed, fitted, balanced wheels also stood up to rough mountain travel as well as the desert heat.

Where were the Conestoga wagons built that were used by emigrants to travel across the state of Wyoming?

Conestoga wagons were named for the valley in Lancaster County, Pennsylvania, where they were built by German settlers. One of the main freight carriers in the East from 1750 until the advent of the railroads, the wagon's boat-shaped body prevented loads from shifting. Because the wagons were custom built, no two were alike. The wagon usually had a vermilion running gear, a Prussian blue wagon body, and a white canvas cover. A team of oxen or four to six horses were required to pull the wagon and wide wheels kept it from getting stuck in the mud. Pennsylvania Mennonites are credited with developing the Conestoga.

What form of transportation was used to haul tons of machinery and building materials to the Pathfinder Dam site from 1905 to 1909?

String teams of horses were used to pull wagons loaded with supplies to the dam site to build the diversion tunnel and reservoir. Teamsters made the trip in as few as three days from Casper, or as many as seventy-six days with heavy equipment and in severe weather.

When did the horseless carriage appear on the scene?

A steam-powered self-propelled vehicle was built by Nicolas Cugnot in 1769, but it wasn't until 1886 that an internal combustion engine was completed by German inventors. Steam, electric, and gasoline-powered autos competed for sales before gasoline-powered engines took over the market in 1910. The first automobile patent was granted to George Selden in 1895, but production-line assembly of affordable cars didn't occur until 1910. The first horseless carriage appeared in Wyoming in 1903 and the first automobile license was issued in 1913 to J.M. Schwoob in Cheyenne. In 1910, a $4,500 fire truck was purchased for the city of Casper, and two years later the first truck replaced string teams to haul equipment to the Salt Creek Oilfield.

How did Wyoming residents dispose of "broomtails?"

Mustangs were rounded up and broken to ride, but after the turn of the twentieth century, the horses were usually sold to the local rendering plants for horsemeat to export to Europe. They were also recycled into poultry feed, cracklings, shoe leather, and grease. Those who rounded them up would receive two cents a pound on the hoof. Young men removed the mufflers from their cars and drove them across the prairie to round up horses. Some automobiles were "high centered" and wrecked in the process.

Which early Wyoming family used their polo field as an aircraft landing strip?

The Wallop family of Big Horn, Wyoming, used their polo field for a landing strip. Oliver Wallop, Senator Malcolm Wallop's father, was one of the pioneer aviators in the nation who operated a flying service in the Big Horn area. He began flying during the early 1920s in canvas-covered, open cockpit planes. His son, Malcolm, also owned his own charter service during the late 1960s and early 1970s, using a Cessna 182 and Beechcraft Baron. The polo field was originally used by horse buyers during the Boer War to judge the gait of the horses they purchased.

How did United States airmail pilots in 1921 stay on course over Wyoming?

Flying during daylight hours, pilots followed maps that listed various sites on the ground. During flights from Omaha to Cheyenne and Salt

Lake City, pilots not only determined the correct compass course, correcting for drift, but kept landmarks in sight. The city of Cheyenne was first identified from the air by the Fort Russell barracks. Pilots then followed the Colorado and Southern Railroad tracks to the federal airport. Those landing in Cheyenne for the first time had to take special care due to the "rarified atmosphere at 6,000 feet," and were instructed to follow the tracks to the first town after they made a sharp bend to the north where the black, irregular peaks of the Laramie Mountains could be seen. The planes then flew over the mountains into the Laramie Valley and on to Salt Lake City.

Which breeds of horses were used for farming on the high plains?

Percherons, Clydesdales, Shires, Belgians, and mixed breeds were mainly used for farming purposes. Usually the teams were not well matched, according to Milt Cunningham, whose father farmed in the Big Horn area. Teams used for hauling employed larger horses as the "swing and wheelers." The leaders were called "feelers" and were lighter and more agile than the larger horses, but usually not trained primarily for pulling. They were used to guide the other horses on snow-packed trails.

Which type of ship was first christened the U.S.S. Wyoming?

The first ship to be named the U.S.S. Wyoming

was a wooden hulled, steam-powered sloop, launched in 1859. The second U.S.S. Wyoming was launched in 1900 in San Francisco and was the first United States vessel converted from coal to oil in 1908. The ship's name was changed to the U.S.S. Cheyenne in 1909, so that a third ship could be named the U.S.S. Wyoming. The third U.S.S. Wyoming was the Atlantic Fleet's flag ship. Commissioned in 1912, the battleship took part in both world wars and was a member of the Sixth Battle Squadron of the "Grand Fleet" during World War I. She was converted to a gunnery training ship during the Second World War.

What type of vessel is classified as a boomer?

The current U.S.S. Wyoming is a trident nuclear submarine, known as a boomer. The boomers are fleet ballistic missile submarines, which carry as many as twenty-four long-range nuclear warhead missiles, an important part of the United States' nuclear defense arsenal.

Wyoming's Representatives

Who were senior U.S. senators?

Francis E. Warren, a Republican, was the first senior senator from Wyoming from 1890 until 1893. He was followed by Clarence D. Clark, a Democrat, from 1893-1917. John B. Kendrick, a Democrat, next held the seat from 1917 until 1933. Another Democrat, Joseph O'Mahoney assumed the seat when Kendrick died in 1933, and served until 1953. Republican, Frank A. Barrett held the seat from 1953 until 1959, and Democrat Gale McGee represented Wyoming in the U.S. senate from 1959 until 1977. His seat was won by Republican, Malcolm Wallop, in 1977 and held until 1995. Craig Thomas then served as senior Republican senator from 1995 until his death in 2007. Republican John Barrasso has served since that time.

Who were the state's junior senators?

Joseph M. Carey was Wyoming's first junior Republican senator from 1890 until 1895. Republican, Francis E. Warren next held the seat from 1895 until 1929. Patrick J. Sullivan, a Republican, then served from 1929 until 1930. Republican, Robert D. Carey next served from 1930-1937, and Democrat Henry H. Schwartz served from 1937-1943. Edward V. Robertson, a Republican, held the office from 1943-1949. He was followed by Lester C. Hunt, a Democrat, from 1949-1954. Edward D. Crippa, Republican, only served during 1954, until Joseph O'Mahoney, a Democrat, took the seat until 1961. Republican, Milward L. Simpson, served from 1962-1967, and Clifford Hansen, Republican, served from 1967 until 1978. Alan K. Simpson, also a Republican, served from 1979-1997. Republican Mike Enzi has served since 1997. John Barrasso has served as junior senator since 2007.

Who have been the only two Wyoming women to serve in the U.S. Congress?

Barbara Cubin, a fifth-generation Wyomingite, served as the first woman congressional representative from 1995 until 2008. The mother of two received her B.S. in chemistry in 1969 from Creighton University.

Cynthia Lummis was elected to the U.S. House of Representatives in 2008. She was raised on her family ranch in Laramie County and graduated from the University of Wyoming with bachelor degrees in Animal Science and Biology. She became the youngest woman elected to the Wyoming Legislature in 1979. In 1985, she received her law degree from the University of Wyoming. Lummis clerked at the Wyoming Supreme Court, then practiced law in Cheyenne, and served a total of fourteen years in the Wyoming House and Senate. She was then elected Wyoming State Treasurer in 1998, and served for eight years before successfully running for the U.S. House of Representatives.

Bibliography

Angler Guide online

Asinah.net Encyclopedia: The Automobile

Nathaniel, Burt, *Compass American Guides, Wyoming,* Brittanica Concise Encyclopedia, Oakland, California, 1991

Canadian Broadcasting Company Archives, "Hudson's Bay Company Ends It's Fur Trade"

Chrisman, Harry E., author, *1001 Most-Asked Questions About the American West,* Swallow Press, Chicago, Illinois, 1962

Dary, David, *Red Blood and Black Ink: Journalism in the Old West,* University Press of Kansas, 1998

Dobler, Lavinia, *I Didn't Know That About Wyoming,* Misty Mountain Press, Selah, Washington, 1986.

Dobler, Lavinia, *Wild Wind, Wild Water*, Misty Mountain Press, Casper, Wyoming, 1983

Eddins, Orland Ned, *Mountains of Stone*, Historical Society and Museum of Jackson Hole, SP, 1998

Fort Phil Kearny Trail Association and Foundation, Story, Wyoming

Fort Osage National Historic Park homepage

GORP, Wyoming Wilderness area, Wyoming

Houston, S., *Wyoming's Railroad History*, Wyoming State Archives

Irving, Washington, *The Adventures of Captain Bonneville or, Scenes beyond the Rocky Mountains of the Far West*, Paris, Galignani, 1837

Jackson Hole, Wyoming, Travel Guide

Karamanski, Theodore J.; *Fur Trade Exploration Opening the Far Northwest 1821-1852*, University of Oklahoma Press, 1999

Karolevitz, Robert F., *Newspapering in the Old West*, Bonanza Books, New York, New York

Mead, Jean Henry, *Casper Country: Wyoming's Heartland*, Medallion Books, Evansville, Wyoming, 2004

Mead, Jean Henry, *Westerners: Candid and Historic Interviews,* Medallion Books, Evansville, Wyoming, 2003.

McWilliams, Mary Ann, The Wyoming State Historic Website

Wyoming Historical Trivia

Mennonite Historical Society

National Park Service webpage

Natrona County Library research librarians

Oregon Trail National Historic Trail homepage

Pence, Richard, *"The Homestead Act of 1862"*

Sierra Club, Wyoming Chapter

State of Wyoming Historical Dates

Statewide Information Services, Wyoming State Library

The GoWyld Webteam by the Wyoming State Library and WYLD Library Consortium

The Big Horn Basin Foundation Dinosaur Center

The Casper Star-Tribune, Casper, Wyoming.

The Northeast Wyoming Development Coalition

Trenholm, Virginia Cole and Carley, Maurine, *The Shoshonis, Sentinels of the Rockies*; University of Oklahoma Press, 1964.

The California Military Museum

The Virtual Museum of the City of San Francisco, "Driving the Last Spike", *San Francisco News Letter*, 1925.

The Worldwide Wickipedia Encyclopedia,

J. J. Hammond

Geophysical Fluid Dynamics Laboratory

University of Wyoming Digital Initiative

Urbanek, Mae, *Wyoming Place Names*, Johnson Publishing, Boulder, Colorado, 1967

U.S. Department of Agriculture, Forest Service

U.S. Department of Agriculture, Natural Resources Conservation Resources Service

U. S. Geological Survey report on earthquakes

U. S. Geological Survey, University of Utah

UnitedStateshistory.com

Utah! Adventure and Travel

Wasden, Winifred Sawaya, *Modern Pioneers*, Northwest College, Powell, WY, 1998

Wheeler, Keith, *The Townspeople*, Time Life Books Western Series, 1975.

Wildernet, Your Guide to Outdoor Recreation

Wyoming Division of State Parks and Cultural Resources

Wyoming Facts and City Index, Key to the City, U.S. City Information

Wyoming Game and Fish Department's Private Lands Public Wildlife Access Program

Wyoming Geological Association, 44th Annual Field Conference Guidebook

Wyoming Press Association, *Wyoming Newspapers. A Centennial History*, Cheyenne, Wyoming, 1990

Wyoming Public Television

Wyoming State Government Website Wyoming State Parks and Historic Sites

Yellowstone Net: The History of Yellowstone Park

www.ingramcontent.com/pod-product-compliance
Lightning Source LLC
Chambersburg PA
CBHW070640050426
42451CB00008B/234